Compelling Buyers to Call

The Realtor's Guide to Attracting Buyers in Today's Market

_____

Loren K. Keim

Loren Keim's Compelling Buyers to Call

Copyright © 2011 Loren K. Keim

All rights reserved. No part of this book shall be reproduced or transmitted in any form or by any means, electronic, mechanical, magnetic, photographic including photocopying, recording or by any information storage and retrieval system, without prior written permission of the publisher. No patent liability is assumed with respect to the use of the information contained herein. Although every precaution has been taken in the preparation of this book, the publisher and the author assume no responsibility for errors or omissions. Neither is any liability assumed for damages resulting from the use of the information contained herein.

ISBN 978-1466433380

Loren Keim's Compelling Buyers to Call

Acknowledgements

The 27 years I've spent as a Real Estate Agent and Broker have been an exciting adventure. The people who have helped me to perfect my prospecting programs are too numerous to mention, but I do want to thank some of the people who have significantly contributed to my programs (while hopefully not leaving anyone important out):

Theresa Keim, Loren Keim Sr, Tim Mahon, Dan Gooder Richard, Michelle Miller, Mike Miller, Ellie Barrett, Wayne Talaber, Mae Gunn, Judy Mazzeo, Marc Lucarelli, Joe Bartera, Pattie Hartman, Deb Hartman, Bonnie Smith, and many others!

I also want to thank the people who assisted me with editing and compiling all this information:

Betty Broadbent, Crystal Franklin and Keri Schlosser.

And, of course, this list wouldn't be complete without acknowledging some of the greatest real estate trainers in the country. I highly recommend anyone reading this book take the time to learn from each of these highly gifted trainers:

Floyd Wickman – www.FloydWickman.com
Joe Stumpf – www.byreferralonly.com
Dr. Dick McKenna – Co Creator of the Orbit Program
Ralph Williams – Co Creator of the Orbit Program

Table of Contents

Contents

Acknowledgements 3

Chapter 1: Shifting Our Paradigm on Buying 11
   The Problem is You 11
   Why Should Renters Buy Homes Now? 13
      The Tipping Point 15
      Why Are Interest Rates SO Important? 20
      But What If Prices Drop? 22
      Why Will Interest Rates Rise? 24
      Qualifying Now VS Later 25
   What is Keeping People from Buying? 26

Chapter 2 - Improving Your Traditional Buyer Attraction Techniques 29
   IDX and VOW feeds 30
   Syndicating Your Listings 32
      Postlets 33
      ListHub 35
      Point2Agent 36
   Adding Virtual Tours 37
   Conclusion 40

Chapter 3 - Shifting Your Paradigm 41
   The Cheese Moves 41
   What IS The Traditional Buyer Business? 42

Loren Keim's Compelling Buyers to Call

Honestly, Why Do We Advertise?..48

Why Doesn't Most Advertising Work? 52

    Image Advertising 52

    Individual Property Advertising 54

Switching..56

    Sign Calls 58

    Newspaper and Magazine Advertisement Calls 61

    Internet Calls 63

Summary 63

Chapter 4 - Compelling Offers and Free Information 65

    What Are Compelling Offers? 65

    Attraction Techniques..68

    Newsworthy Marketing 71

    Free Reports..72

        Gooder Group 77

    Free Reports on the Internet 78

    Market Evaluations 81

    Automatic Listing Updates...83

    Summary 85

Chapter 5 - Target Markets and Unique Selling Propositions 87

    Selecting Your Target Market 87

    A Sampling of Buyer Prospecting Markets 91

    Target Markets by Specific Type of Property..............................93

Loren Keim's Compelling Buyers to Call

Using a USP – Unique Selling Proposition 94

    1 – Niche Market USP 95

    2 – Unique Service USP 96

    3 – Service or Performance Guarantee 97

    4 – Comparison USP 97

Summary 98

Chapter 6 - Delivering Your Message 101

    The Delivery System for Your Message 102

    Mailing 102

        Letters VS Postcards 103

        Emotional Response 104

        Testimonials and Evidence of Success Mailings 107

        Newsletters 109

    E-Newsletters and Email 110

        Email Tag Lines 111

    Business Cards 112

    Attracting with Promotional Products 112

    Specialized or Targeted Web Sites 116

Chapter 7 - Social Media Platforms and Video 123

    The Rules of Engagement 125

    Facebook 126

        Creating a Profile 126

        Building a Network and Finding Friends 126

Loren Keim's Compelling Buyers to Call

News feeds and Your Wall 128
Posting Events 133
Direct Response and Facebook 134
Ads and Pages 134
Targeted Advertising on Facebook 135
Twitter 137
LinkedIn 139
ActiveRain and Broker Agent Social 141
Other Social Media Sites 142
Viral Video Marketing 143
The Next Level of Viral Video 145
Summary 146

Chapter 8 - Utilizing Mortgage Products to Attract Buyers 147
Low Down Payment Loans 149
Are there 100% financed loans? 151
Rural Housing 152
VA Loans 154
Navy Federal 154
Community Reinvestment Loans 155
Voice Mail Capture Systems 155
The Bright Yellow Sign Campaign 160
The Classified Campaign 162
Online Classified Campaign 165
The Laundry Flyer Campaign 165

Loren Keim's Compelling Buyers to Call

The Apartment Flyer Campaign 166

Offers from Lenders 167

In Summary 168

Chapter 9 – Sphere of Influence and Past Clients 171

Creating Your Sphere of Influence List 180

Memory Teasers 181

In Summary 186

Chapter 10 - Follow-Up Systems 189

Handling each type of buyer 192

Systems 194

Client Databases 195

Drip Systems 197

Creating Action Plans 198

ADDING TO YOUR DATABASE 202

Auto Responders 202

Humor 204

A Final Word on Contact Management 205

Chapter 11 - Buyer Presentations – Step by Step 207

The Presentation 208

Summary 218

Chapter 12 - Getting Referrals during the Process 219

The Reticular Activator 220

Loren Keim's Compelling Buyers to Call

Letting Buyers Know We Need Their Help..................................221
Third Party Endorsements 223
Referrals from Exceptional Service 224
    Keeping in Touch..225
    Balloons and Coffee Mugs 225
    Grocery Store Boxes 226
Thanking Your Customer 226
After sale follow up..227
Some Final Thoughts - Change is Inevitable 228
Treating your Business LIKE a Business 229

Index 230
End Notes..240

Chapter 1: Shifting Our Paradigm on Buying

The Problem is You

The book you hold in your hands will outline positive and proactive steps you should take to build your real estate career in the current market, despite the existing challenges, and to grow your personal business to the next level. I feel it is imperative, however, to start with one simple negative thought to help you understand your *need* to change. You're probably not currently selling as many properties as you'd like. Most Realtors are not, and the reason you're not selling as many properties as you'd like is *not* the fault of the market, the economy, the time of the year, the position of the moon and stars, your ex-spouse or your broker. Your income is not being dictated by outside forces. The problem is you. I realize that sounds harsh and unfair, but it's also true.

There are three primary reasons you're not selling as many homes as you'd like. In the last few weeks, I have been to Las Vegas, Chicago, Pittsburgh, Rehoboth Beach, Saint Louis, and I'm on my way to speak in Grand Cayman, among others. Despite being on the road talking

Loren Keim's Compelling Buyers to Call

to audiences, I managed to sell more than ten homes this month, in one of the worst markets in history, in only a few days of work.

I am not bragging. Rather I am trying to convince you that selling five, ten or fifteen homes each month can be done, *in spite* of the market. Further, I do *not* have the *'gift of gab'* and I don't currently represent any builders. I don't have all the foreclosed homes in my area listed and I don't have dozens of investors. What I have is a burning desire to help people. We all need to understand and believe that consumers *want* to own homes. They do. They are afraid to make a move and need education and guidance to help them step over the fence into becoming home owners. But first we need to identify those people who really want to buy.

Let's get back to my original statement. The reason you're not selling as many homes as you'd like in this market is you. There are three major reasons, components or attitudes that are holding you back from being the person I know you can be. The first is your subconscious belief that you may be doing a buyer a disservice by selling them a home when home prices may fall again. That is patently false, and I will outline why in the next few sections.

The second is that you believe there are no *real* buyers in the market. You believe, like many buyers, that no one can qualify for a mortgage since lending restrictions have tightened and those buyers who *do* qualify are out to bruise and abuse you. This attitude comes from your experience over the past two years. I'm going to show you how you can attract dozens of potential buyers, allowing you to pick and choose who you'd like to work with, and convince you that mortgages are attainable. You have to carefully qualify those buyers and then work to bullet-proof the transaction.

Finally, you're depressed about your income and the market and you're not working in your career as if it's a true full time job. Get off the

Loren Keim's Compelling Buyers to Call

sofa and put down the bag of Doritos, because we're going to need to roll up our sleeves and get to work.

"Loren," you might say, "what is all this touchy feely crap? It's not like you. I need to sell a house so I can pay my mortgage and my car payment this month. All I really want is a tip or a technique that will attract buyers to buy homes today." I understand, but techniques only work if you truly believe in them and understand *why* they work. You have to change your attitude and perhaps your beliefs and *then* take action in order to take full advantage of the program I'm going to lay out in this book.

Why Should Renters Buy Homes Now?

First, you have to understand that owning a home is a great investment and that assisting customers to purchase homes is in their best interest. The last few years of declining real estate prices have programmed too many Realtors to believe that they are doing a disservice to the public by representing them in the purchase of homes.

If you don't believe you're truly helping your clients, it will come through to them in your actions. A few months ago, I was shocked as I listened to one of the agents in my firm tell a buyer that if they wanted to save money for a year or two for a bigger down payment, that might be a good move because housing prices might even go lower. I'm hoping to show you why that may be the worst advice you can give a potential future home owner.

Last year, I wrote an article for *Broker Agent Social* about buyer's remorse. I explained how an agent might effectively discuss normal home buying fears with their clients in order to ease the client's concern about purchasing a home. Although the feedback on the article was mostly

Loren Keim's Compelling Buyers to Call

positive, the online version of the article received negative comments. Some Realtors argued that we should be encouraging buyers to take the purchase more seriously and actively try to talk them out of buying because prices will fall and more buyers will be upside down with their mortgages, stuck in homes they can't even give away on their way to foreclosure because they're buried in the debt and the world will end in a ball of fire as the moon... ah, but I digress. Some Realtors actually wrote that they felt guilty because they were, in effect, cheating the public by selling them a declining asset. I was shocked by Realtors who honestly believed the dream of home ownership would be a nightmare forever.

Let's look at it a little differently. Isn't it true that when we buy cars, most of us look less at the sticker price than at what the car is actually going to cost us during the five years we own it? We weigh that option of buying a car with a car-loan rather than lease the car. Why do some people purchase time-shares? Is it because time-shares appreciate in value? Not very likely. We buy time-shares in order to lock in our vacations at a lower price than we'll be paying in the future.

We buy homes for many reasons. We buy them so we can pick and choose our own colors, so we have a sense of security, so we can have a permanent place to raise our families that is *not* subject to a landlord selling the home out from under us. We buy homes so that we can lock in our future payments, rather than be at the mercy of inflation and rent increases. And we buy homes in order to have no house payment thirty years from now when we're ready to retire and we're on fixed incomes.

Sadly, we have very short memories. We tend only to consider the last few years when prices fell and when many of our friends and neighbors lost their homes because they lost their incomes and couldn't keep up with the payments. Historically, home ownership has been one of the best investments an individual or family can make for their retirement, and historically interest rates have been much higher than they are today.

There have always been people losing their jobs due to the economy, factory shut-downs or illness. The difference in the recent past is that housing prices fell so precipitously in many parts of the country that home owners couldn't simply sell their homes to pay off the mortgages. They had to renegotiate their payoffs through a short sale, or they had to walk away from the home leaving it to foreclosure. What we forget is that market corrections have happened throughout history, and although this is one of the worst we've faced over the last century, it's not unique, and like the roller-coaster of life, the market will, at some point, reverse direction and improve. In fact, I believe we're going to begin seeing improvement over the next year.

If truth be told, we all know that those who will be real estate rich a decade from now are the ones who will purchase the most property at the bottom of the market, don't we? The question might be - how can we time the market, and I want to suggest that we don't have to, because now is a great time to buy.

The Tipping Point

In the *New York Times* best-selling book, T*he Tipping Point*, Malcolm Gladwell made a strong case for the concept that there is a point where an idea, a trend or a behavior reaches explosive growth. "Just as a single sick person can start an epidemic of the flu,"[i] the right combination of factors can lead a large segment of the population to form the same belief or move in the same direction.

In the real estate market, this effect can be seen in several drastic upswings and collapses of the market over the past hundred years. Didn't it seem like everyone decided in 2005 and 2006 that 'now' was the best

Loren Keim's Compelling Buyers to Call

time to buy a home? People rushed out to buy despite rapidly rising housing prices, afraid they'd be priced out of the market, as if the upswing would never end. While it's true that much of the real estate boom can be attributed to easy credit and low interest rates, there's a quieter factor as well that builds with the phenomenon of a real estate boom. It's the emotional need of consumers to follow others or be like others. If Bob and Sally were buying a bigger, fancier home, and the payment isn't drastically higher than their moderate home's payment, then their friends should too.

The momentum of the market builds until we reach a tipping point in the market when a significant portion of the population rushes out to purchase. I first experienced this early in my career in 1986 through 1988, which was followed by a significant crash in our market from 1989 through 1993. The same philosophy occurs in reverse when the public thinks we're headed for a crash. We see this during major stock sell-offs on the stock market.

When the real estate market began to fall in 2007, economic factors were still very good. Employment was relatively high, the population was expanding, thereby increasing the demand for housing stock and interest rates were extremely low in a historical context. While the market had overinflated, and while a percentage of the market had used subprime loans to purchase above their means, the factors were not in place for the greatest real estate crash since the great depression. Yet, we all saw it happen.

Certainly there were, and still are, some significant issues with our economy and with our government's "spend-spend-spend" economic policy. But news reports that outlined how prices would fall by huge percentages were pivotal factors creating enough panic that those who would normally have purchased homes dropped completely out of the market, creating a self-fulfilled prophecy.

Loren Keim's Compelling Buyers to Call

Today, negative press, political posturing, and stories of neighbors being foreclosed have coalesced to create the illusion that buying a home is a bad investment. Worse, a large percentage of the population believes they can't purchase a home because either banks aren't lending and mortgage funds are not available or that mortgage restrictions are so high that potential buyers will not qualify without twenty or more percent down and perfect credit. As Realtors or mortgage originators, we all know that a first time buyer can purchase a home through FHA financing with only 3.5% down payment and a credit score in the mid to low 600's (at least at the point I'm writing this book), but the general public does not.

Although the majority of the public can purchase a home with this kind of financing, the illusion that they can't get mortgages is so prevalent that potential buyers don't want to even try, for fear of embarrassment. This situation is aggravated by articles that suggest prices could fall an additional ten percent or more.

Remember that at the very peak of the market, while some were screaming hysterically that the housing bubble was ready to burst, others were protesting that all real estate was local and that rapidly rising housing prices were actually a function of our fast paced society and our mobility. Many so-called experts argued, just before the crash, that home prices had plenty of room to grow before slowing. As your mother probably told you when you were small, don't believe everything you read.

Now there are reporters and politicians telling us that real estate will never rise again and, in fact, will drop another ten, twenty or fifty percent before the bottom is reached. There is shadow inventory secretly held by the banks and every other person is defaulting and prices will plunge for the next decade.

Loren Keim's Compelling Buyers to Call

These purveyors of doom are ignoring some fundamental truths. The population is continuing to expand rapidly. Part of this expansion is the result of immigration and part is attributed to birth rates and seniors living longer. A growing population means an increased demand for housing for that population which ultimately leads to prices rising. Supply and demand are a fundamental part of economics. Higher demand for any fixed commodity leads to a higher price. This need for housing has been buffered by families doubling up during the recession. Kids are staying longer with parents or parents are moving in with their kids. That dynamic will change as the economy recovers.

Additionally, the Federal Reserve printing a lot of paper money means we dilute and devalue the dollar, which leads to inflation. Although inflation creates higher interest rates, which is bad for the housing market, it also means that everything you buy costs more and housing will inevitably follow that pattern.

So, while we hear there will never be another real estate boom, we know this is untrue. There will be another tipping point in the market, because history repeats itself and our memories are painfully short. And I repeat: those who will be real estate rich during the next boom are those who are buying now.

Another consideration is that people are leaping to buy gold right now because they see gold as a real tangible asset rather than paper money. Isn't real estate also a tangible asset? Isn't real estate, if purchased correctly, a solid investment that cannot go to zero like General Motors stock or many other bankrupt too-big-to-fail companies did? If a home is purchased at a low enough payment that it can easily be rented at or below the mortgage payment, you can weather any storm with a real estate asset by simply renting the home.

Let's re-examine the reasons why we buy homes. Although historically homes have been a great investment and retirement plan,

Loren Keim's Compelling Buyers to Call

that's not the primary reason we buy. We buy to both lock in our housing cost and to secure something that is truly ours. A mentor of mine, Ralph Williams, once told me that real estate is the tip of the iceberg of free society. If you can't own your own land, and are required to lease it from some government or third party as a serf would, you can't truly be free.

We buy homes, even when the monthly cost of home ownership may be a bit higher than current rental rates, because we know that the cost of rent will continue to rise. And in many parts of the country, the monthly payment on a median priced home is less than a monthly rental on the same type of home. If rents follow inflation, and rises at a very low 2.5% each year, in twenty years your $1000 rental payment will be nearly $1600 a month, based on compounding interest. In thirty years, when you'd be paying off your home if you took out a thirty year mortgage, your rent would be over $2000 and keep rising until you die, leaving no home as part of your estate.

If inflation is a more realistic 3.5% to 4% over the next few decades, your $1000 rent payment will go to $1922 per month in twenty years at 3.5% or $2106 per month at 4%. In thirty years, you'll be paying $2711 at 3.5% inflation and a huge $3118 if inflation adjustments to rent are at 4%, while your home would be paid off.

Let's say our government policy to "spend-spend-spend" leads us to inflation of 7%, which is still far below the inflation rates of the late 1970's and early 1980's, that means your rent will jump from $1000 to $3616 in year twenty and $7114 in year thirty when you're looking to retire. If you bought a home with a $1200 mortgage payment in that first year, your payment would still be $1200 until it's paid off, other than increases in property taxes.

Loren Keim's Compelling Buyers to Call

	2.5% Inflation	3.5% Inflation	7% Inflation	Mortgage Payment
Year 1	$1,000.00	$1,000.00	$1,000.00	$1,200.00
Year 10	$1,248.86	$1,362.90	$1,838.46	$1,200.00
Year 20	$1,598.65	$1,922.50	$3,616.53	$1,200.00
Year 30	$2,046.41	$2,711.88	$3,118.65	$1,200.00
Year 31	$2,097.57	$2,806.79	$7,612.26	$0.00

Why Are Interest Rates SO Important?

Interest rates are the other key to why buyers should be buying today. Although fluctuating on a daily basis, rates have been in the mid 4% range lately for a thirty year fixed rate loan to a borrower with decent credit. Obviously rates can be different depending on someone's credit score, on their down payment, on the term of the loan taken and so forth, but let's use a typical thirty year 10% down conventional loan at 4.875% as the basis for our discussion, which is higher than the current rate as I write this book.

Due to the public's fear and panic over falling real estate prices, and the significant impact of foreclosures in the last two years, I believe the market has over-corrected. As a percentage of income, it is actually cheaper to buy the median home today, in many parts of the country, than at any point since the 1950's. When my firm first opened in Allentown, Pennsylvania in the early 1980's, interest rates were around 17%. Further back in the late 1960's and early 1970's, rates were north of 8%. That is double the payment of a 4% loan for the same money. Even when the market boomed in the late 1980's, rates were higher than 8% and, at many points, higher than 10%.

Inflation has made housing prices higher today than the 1970's, 80's and 90's, obviously, but it has also made our incomes significantly higher than our parents and grandparents from those eras. Since home prices have fallen over the past few years, and rates have remained historically low, you can borrow money and buy the median home, in

Loren Keim's Compelling Buyers to Call

many parts of the country, with a payment of only 14 to 20 percent of your gross monthly income. That's far below the percentage of monthly income we've spent in prior decades to own real estate.

The key factor I'm trying to get across is that you buy a home and lock in a payment, and as long as you aren't transferred to another region of the country, the immediate home value doesn't matter nearly as much as that payment, because over the long-term, values will rise.

I believe that rates will rise. Many experts and economists agree with me. The question is how much will they rise. For those readers who are screaming that rates will not rise, I'll address that in the next section. Depending on inflation, rates may rise only 1% over the next year, or they may rise 3 to 5% over the next two years. If we hit some sort of hyperinflation, based on our country's borrowing habits, all bets on inflating interest rates are off.

What does this mean on a typical home purchase? If you purchased a $200,000 home with a 10% down payment, your mortgage payment would be $952.57 per month plus property taxes and insurance. Again, this is based on a thirty year loan. If rates rise just 1% over the next year and your buyer waits to purchase, that same payment will be $1064.77 per month, which is $112 more per month or $1346 more in payments per year and adds up to over $40,000 during the term of the loan in additional payments.

If rates rise 3% in the next eighteen months, as some predict, that same mortgage will then cost $1305.12 per month, a whopping $352.55 per month more than they'd pay today or another $126,918 in additional interest over the life of the loan.

Loren Keim's Compelling Buyers to Call

> ### $200,000 Home Purchase
>
> At 4.875%, Payment is $952.57 per month
>
> At 5.875%, Payment is $1064.77 ($112 more per month or $1346 per year, over $40,000 for the term of the loan.
>
> At 7.875%, Payment is $1305.12 ($352.55 per month more, or another $126,918)
>
> - Based on 10% down 30 year mortgage
> - Payment does not include taxes, insurance and MIP

I also have trouble believing that the majority of potential future home buyers realize they can own a $200,000 home for less than a thousand a month (before taxes and insurance). How much will they pay to lease the same home? How much will they pay to lease that home in ten years?

Let's go to an extreme. Let's say interest rates spike back to 10%, where they had been for many years before this current period of exceptionally low rates. At 10%, that same $952.57 mortgage payment would cost $1579.63, which is $627.06 more per month or $225,741 more in payments over the life of the loan.

But What If Prices Drop?

If I were a gambler I'd bet against any more significant drops in housing prices because, although there are many foreclosures yet to dump onto the market, the number of borrowers going into default has been dropping and the unemployment rate has been dropping. It is a

Loren Keim's Compelling Buyers to Call

valid concern, however. No one wants to pay $200,000 for a home today and find it to be worth ten percent less next year.

Let's select a Midwestern suburban area where housing prices have dropped 21% over the past five years. This is a typical scenario across the country. There are areas that have been hit much harder, such as Las Vegas and Orlando, but we're looking for the normal market. If the average price drop was about 4% per year and some segments of the economy are improving, it's reasonable to assume a drop wouldn't exceed 4%.

A buyer of a $200,000 home could lose $8000 in equity if prices erode another 4% over the next year. Yet, if that buyer stays in the home as the market recovers, he will recoup that equity. But what if he could buy today at a 4.875% interest rate, and waiting a year cost him a 1% increase in that interest rate? The $200,000 purchase would cost $952.57 per month, again based on a thirty year loan with ten percent down payment. Buying the same home for $192,000 next year, but at a rate of 5.875%, will actually cost him $1022.18 per month, nearly $70 more per month even though he's paying less for the home. If rates spike to 7.875%, that same home, now at only $192,000, will cost $1252.92 per month, more than $300 more per month for a lower priced home.

Now what if your gamble of waiting doesn't pay off and both prices

What if Prices Drop??

- They've dropped 21% over <u>5</u> years. IF they drop another 4%...
- $200,000 Home costs $952.57 per month.
- $192,000 (4% less) at 5.875% is $1022.18
- $192,000 at 7.875% is $1252.92

- Based on 10% down 30 year mortgage
- Payment does not include taxes, insurance and MIP

Loren Keim's Compelling Buyers to Call

and interest rates rise?

Why Will Interest Rates Rise?

As I warn of the potential of rising interest rates at workshops around the country, I inevitably get someone in the audience who argues. "Loren," they begin, "interest rates will not rise because the government can't allow it." Here's a newsflash - the government doesn't control home mortgage interest rates. The government can influence them for a period of time, but cannot set the rate.

There are two parties to every mortgage. There is the borrower and there is the organization who loans the money to the borrower. For a bank or individual to loan money to another, they have to receive some benefit for loaning that money, and that is the interest paid by the borrower. Although that may sound simplistic, the way the real world works is that large organizations, like Fannie Mae, buy up billions of dollars in mortgages, package them as Mortgage Backed Securities and resell them on the secondary market to investors. If banks and Fannie Mae can't get the loans sold, the supply of money goes down, meaning there is less money to lend, which drives rates up. I'm oversimplifying, of course, but that's the basic way mortgages work.

Mortgage rates change based on the interest rates paid by Federal Treasuries and by inflation. Treasuries are considered to be the safest investments in the world because they are backed by "the full faith and credit" of the United States government, meaning the risk of default is very low. Unlike U.S. Treasury bills and Treasury bonds, mortgages are certainly not risk-free, meaning that we entice investors to purchase mortgages by offering a higher rate than treasuries, based on a risk-factor.

Loren Keim's Compelling Buyers to Call

Treasury rates have to also be higher than inflation or an investor will lose money. For example, if an investor purchases a Treasury bond that pays 3% interest, but inflation is 4%, the investment is not keeping up with inflation and the bond will be worth less at the end than it was in the beginning. Mortgage rates must be higher than Treasury rates, which must be higher than inflation, or the loans cannot be sold and borrowers will have a difficult time obtaining financing for their home.

The two primary reasons that mortgage rates have held so low for this extended period is that inflation has been virtually non-existent and the Fed has been purchasing bonds in order to influence the rates, keeping them artificially low. As this eases, rates will necessarily rise.

Qualifying Now VS Later

A final thought on the interest rates. As rates rise, consumer's buying power diminishes. For example, a typical family earning $50,000 per year can afford a payment of $1166 per month if we use a qualifying ratio of 28% of their gross monthly income. If we estimate $300 in taxes and insurance, which certainly depends on state and location of the property, their mortgage principal and interest can't exceed $866 per month.

While $866 gives this family the buying power to borrow a $163,700 mortgage if the rate is 4.875%, it means they can only borrow $146,283 if rates go up by only 1%. If rates jump 3% over the next eighteen months, their ability to borrow is now reduced to less than a $120,000 mortgage, while they qualify for $163,700 today.

$50,000 income

- $866 will buy a $163,700 mortgage at 4.875%

- $866 will buy a $146,283 mortgage at 5.875%

- $866 will only buy a $119,448 mortgage at 7.875% – you lose purchase power as rates increase.

- Based on 10% down 30 year mortgage without property taxes or insurance.

What is Keeping People from Buying?

Certainly there are fewer consumers in the marketplace that qualify to purchase a home than a few years ago. Credit scores have dropped for those who let homes go to foreclosure, or gave them back to lenders as a deed-in-lieu or sold their homes through a short sale to get out. Restrictions on lending have tightened as well. PMI companies are scrutinizing transactions and lenders are requiring higher credit scores and more money down.

Effectively that means there are fewer potential buyers than perhaps there were in 2006, but the hidden truth is that the vast majority of Americans can still buy a home. The key to unlocking the floodgates of buyers is to entice first time buyers to make the leap into home ownership. In a normal market, first time buyers generate three or more transactions. They purchase a home, leading the owner of that home to move up to a moderate priced home. That owner, in turn, makes a lateral move to another area or moves up to buy a luxury home, and that luxury home owner may move to a smaller home for retirement.

Loren Keim's Compelling Buyers to Call

In addition to the challenge that there were fewer first time buyers taking the plunge into home ownership over the past two years, many of those first time buyers who actually purchased homes were able to find foreclosures or short-sales which are both homes where the prior owner is unlikely to buy another home. So the chain of transactions ends with the first sale.

Right now, many of these potential first-time buyers are sitting on the sideline. Consumers overwhelmingly want to own their own home rather than throw money away to a landlord, and yet they're not making a move to home ownership. Some are waiting for another tax credit which will probably never come. Some are waiting for a drop in interest rates, which is even less likely. And still others are waiting for the government to give houses away for free. Just listen to some of the recent protestors on Wall Street.

The more rational consumers are not buying because of fear. These fears include falling prices, mortgage qualifications and lack of disposable income in case of some unexpected expenses of home ownership. They worry that prices will fall further because everyone knows someone who took a terrible hit in the current real estate depression, and let's face facts - it *has* been a real estate depression.

Buyers have a fear they won't qualify for a mortgage. As I mentioned earlier, many don't even want to try because they don't want to be embarrassed applying for a mortgage. They've heard from family members, friends and co-workers that it's nearly impossible to get a mortgage, and although that is absolutely not true, they don't want to apply for a mortgage and be denied.

Finally, disposable income has been a real concern. Buyers don't feel as wealthy since they pay seventy or eighty dollars to fill up their gas tank, have higher utility and grocery bills, receive no return on their savings account and watch money evaporate in the stock market.

Loren Keim's Compelling Buyers to Call

What we need to do, as Realtors and mortgage originators, is to identify those who would truly love to own a home but are held back by these fears. Once we identify those potential buyers, we can work toward helping them achieve the dream of home ownership by assisting them in overcoming those fears and in making decisions that will affect them positively.

Where do we go from here? In the next chapter, we'll go over ways to help you improve your success with traditional marketing. Then in the third chapter, we'll attempt to rock your world by showing you alternate methods of attracting buyers. Once you understand how to attract potential buyers and entice them to identify themselves to you, we can work on how to change buyer's perspectives or help to shift their personal paradigm. Finally, we'll create a system of follow-up which will separate you from the gaggle of real estate agents flooding most marketplaces and position yourself as the expert that every buyer *must* have to represent them in the purchase of their home.

Chapter 2 - Improving Your Traditional Buyer Attraction Techniques

Historically, there are two principal sources of potential buyer leads that are not driven by your sphere of influence. One method is to directly market for buyers, which most agents have difficulty with. The more obvious form of buyer attraction is having homes on the market for sale. Super-trainer Floyd Wickman is famous for calling real estate an 'inventory business',[ii] where if you fail to list, you don't last in the industry. Buyers who are in the market are likely to search the internet, drive by 'for sale' signs, go to open houses and pick up homes magazines.

Although we're going to examine methods to attract buyers regardless of whether or not you have listings, and more importantly, to identify potential buyers who may not be in the market to buy currently, we want to improve the number of leads we get from traditional sources as well. Currently, our research shows that the greatest number of buyers generated by Realtors, that are not referred to the Realtor, come in the form of Internet leads. Sign calls are the second highest form and print media advertising calls are fading quickly.

Loren Keim's Compelling Buyers to Call

Of course, we all advertise our listings on the Internet, don't we? Our local Association of Realtors probably puts the listings on their website and on Realtor.com. So why does it matter if you don't spend time carefully editing the language in your online property ad, or spend time adding your listings to other sites? Your properties are already on a few sites, right?

According to comScore Media Metrix, in a study done for Realtor.com in April of 2011, the total number of page views just on Realtor.com, Trulia, Zillow, Yahoo Real Estate and Homes.com exceeded 3.15 billion page views accounting for almost 2 billion minutes spent *just* on these five real estate sites just during the month of April! If we added Century21.com, Re/Max.com, ColdwellBanker.com, FrontDoor, OpenHouse, HomeFinder and a few dozen other top sites to our list, how much time do you believe clients are spending online looking at homes?

Buyers aren't spending as much time driving through neighborhoods anymore because they're shopping online and looking at interior photos in order to eliminate those they don't want to see. If you're not carefully checking your online listings and getting them everywhere possible, you're missing potential buyers.

While some Realtor Associations and real estate franchises syndicate listings for their members to major real estate sites or allow sites to pull the information on your listings, you need to be certain your listings are in all the primary places a buyer is likely to find them.

IDX and VOW feeds

Many Realtors are having difficulty with all the acronyms currently being bantered about the real estate industry. Our first stop on making certain that our listings are available to everyone searching the world wide web is to check with our local MLS to see if our company and our listings are properly set up to be broadcast to internet sites.

Loren Keim's Compelling Buyers to Call

The most common term for allowing our listings to be placed on websites is IDX feed or Internet Data Exchange feed. This system of IDX feeds is often referred to as broker reciprocity, or the sharing of listings between brokerage firms.

There are two ways IDX feeds work. First, you can request an IDX feed from your local MLS for your personal or company website. This will allow you to post all, or at least most of, the MLS listings on your website as if they are yours. The benefit, of course, is that more inventory for a buyer to look at means they're more likely to contact you about a property. Additionally, if buyers find your site easy to navigate and realize they can search the entire MLS from your site, they're more likely to come back again. Some Multiple Listing Services charge for the use of IDX feeds.

The second use of an IDX feed is to allow other brokers to show your listings on their company or personal websites. Larger franchises like Century 21, Re/max, Coldwell Banker and Keller Williams have many IDX feeds which allow the franchises to show consumers every home that is for sale rather than just those for sale with the franchise. In order for your listings to appear on other broker's sites and on the large franchise sites, most Multiple Listing Services require your broker to sign an opt-in agreement with the MLS. If your broker hasn't done this, you may be missing out on having your listings in many more locations.

Although some brokers don't like the idea that their competitors may pick up a buyer from your listing, if your listing isn't on that broker's site, the 'perfect' buyer for that home may not find out that it's for sale. It's similar to a home seller not allowing a 'for sale' sign in their front yard. We need to have the maximum exposure for our properties.

A VOW is a little different than an IDX feed. While IDX feeds provide sites with a limited set of information about each property for sale, a VOW, or Virtual Office Website feed, publishes information

Loren Keim's Compelling Buyers to Call

normally only available to real estate broker's clients. The difference typically is that any consumer can see all the information of an IDX feed on the Internet without registering for the information. VOW feeds require that the viewer register and validate their email address in order to receive the information.

Syndicating Your Listings

Again, web exposure for your listings is critical for two reasons. First, in a competitive situation, you're more likely to list a property if you can visually show the prospective home seller that you place their home for sale on dozens or hundreds of sites rather than just a few. Secondly, the more places that potential buyers can find your listings online, the more likely you are to get buyer inquiries.

Once you've determined that your listings are getting the best exposure possible through your local MLS, you should determine the quickest and most effective route to getting your listings on every other real estate site possible without spending a small fortune. Many great real estate sites like Zillow, Trulia, Craigslist and many others allow you to create a free account and add your listings. I *really* wouldn't recommend spending all day typing listings into hundreds of sites.

The solution is found in using software to submit your properties to multiple sites simultaneously. This is called syndication of your listings. There are dozens of sites that will syndicate your listings. Many of these are free services with the potential for upgrading to more professional versions. The two sites I recommend currently are Postlets and ListHub. Either has a free component that syndicates your properties for sale to many sites and both offer upgrade versions.

Loren Keim's Compelling Buyers to Call

Postlets

    Setting up an account on Postlets[iii] is quick, free and relatively painless. The service is provided by Zillow and allows a Realtor to create a multipage online brochure for a property. These listings are then automatically syndicated to several top real estate sites, and according to the site: "you get all this for the low, low price of zero. Zip. Zilch. Nada."

    Sites that are syndication partners of Postlets, as of the writing of this book, include Enormo, FrontDoor, HotPads, Local, Lycos, Oodle, Overstock, Trulia, Vast, Yahoo Real Estate and Zillow. Additionally, once an online brochure is created for a listing, you can directly post it to Craigslist and to social media sites.

Loren Keim's Compelling Buyers to Call

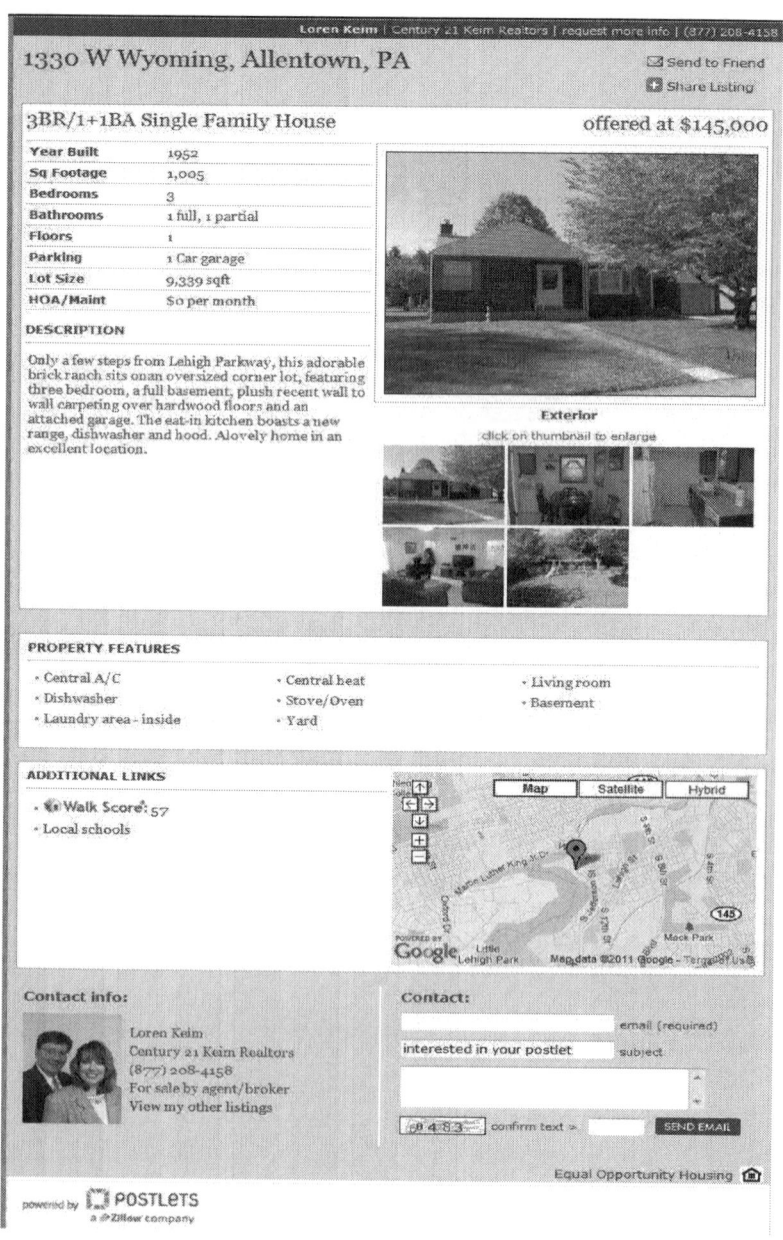

Chapter 2　　　　　　　　　　　　　　　　　　　　　　　　　　　Page 34

Loren Keim's Compelling Buyers to Call

These free online brochures are attractive and interactive. Each may contain multiple photos, a location map, mortgage calculator and Realtor information, as pictured in the sample on the previous page. And the best part is that these beautiful advertisements can be crafted in mere minutes.

With a few keystrokes, the full brochure above can be displayed on Craigslist or you may post a photo link to the brochure on Facebook,

LinkedIn, or dozens of other social media sites.

ListHub

ListHub is the preferred syndication tool for many MLSs, brokerage firms and franchises. Offering a free version as well as an expanded fee version, ListHub had more than 25,000 companies with their own accounts as of mid 2011.

In fact, over three

hundred Multiple Listing Systems are using the service as a syndication partner. In addition, ListHub powers the Fannie Mae online marketing strategy, syndicating their properties to dozens of sites.

The MLS connected service actually requires no data entry or administrative maintenance for users. Additionally, ListHub distributes listings to over fifty national web sites, giving your listing inventory broad exposure to other sites.

Syndication partners with ListHub include Zillow, Yahoo Real Estate, AOL Real Estate, RealtyTrac, openhouse, FrontDoor, Vast, Lycos, LandWatch, National Relocation, Home Finder, Trulia, Hotpads, Enormo, Homes.com, Property Shark and many others.

Point2Agent

Another popular syndication site is Point2Agent. The company offers free listing syndication services to Multiple Listing Services. The information for syndication is automatically pulled from the MLS, like an IDX feed, and syndicated to dozens of other sites. As of the writing of this book, the site is syndicating to more than forty-five national web sites. Point2Agent offers Realtors a variety of tools for a monthly fee.

Remember, just because I'm mentioning a couple syndication sites doesn't mean you shouldn't investigate sites on your own and find the best that works for you. In this fast paced Internet age, what is on top today might be three steps behind next year. Keep your eyes open for future opportunities.

Loren Keim's Compelling Buyers to Call

Adding Virtual Tours

You may be staring at this page, wondering how I could even consider asking you to spend more money on virtual tours when we're in a down economy. You're spending too much already on marketing homes, not to mention the time it would take you to put together a tour on each listing when all you really want is a buyer. The simple truth is that virtual tours attract more buyers to view your listings and they are relatively inexpensive. The two virtual tour software programs my team uses are VisualTour and FirstHomeTour. Both systems are less than thirty dollars a month for an unlimited number of tours, at the writing of this book. If you have five listings, ten listings or one hundred listings, you're still paying a flat fee.

According to Realtor.com, listings with a featured tour are viewed 150% more often than listings without a featured tour. More views lead

Loren Keim's Compelling Buyers to Call

to more prospective buyers contacting you to purchase a home. Is it worth thirty dollars to more than double the number of potential buyers looking at your listings?

Additionally, virtual tour companies like VisualTour and FirstHomeTour actually syndicate your listings for you. Utilizing VisualTour, for example, you can syndicate to Trulia and Zillow and still create sharp ads to post on Craigslist and Facebook in minutes.

Virtual tours are also not as complicated to photograph and build today as they were a few years ago. Many of the software programs allow you to simply shoot still photos, upload them to the virtual tour software and the program will create a video-like presentation out of the still photos. Photos are panned as if you were shooting with a video camera.

In fact, the majority of virtual tours our team builds take less than fifteen minutes. The most challenging part is determining in which order to place the photos and what text to include as captions.

Circular photos were the rage a few years ago but required special equipment and software to create them. VisualTour, as an example, has a built-in processor that allows you to "stitch" photos together and create the same panoramic effect or circular tour effect.

An example can be seen on the next page.

Loren Keim's Compelling Buyers to Call

One other strategy for using virtual tours to attract clients is to send a copy of the virtual tour to your property owner and ask them to forward that virtual tour on to everyone in their own personal email list. They might also add the virtual tour to their Facebook page. Their goal is to sell their home and the more people who know about it being for sale, the more likely a buyer will appear.

"Mrs. Bishwatty, I put your home on one thousand websites and built a beautiful virtual tour of the home in order to attract buyers. You can help us as well. We have no idea who will be the ultimate buyer, but our goal is to get your home in front of as many potential buyers as possible. With that in mind, would you do me a favor? Will you post your home's virtual tour on your Facebook page and send out a link to the tour to everyone in your email list? Ask them if they'll repost it as well. The more people who know about your home, the more likely we are to sell it quickly and for the most money possible."

Loren Keim's Compelling Buyers to Call

Not only is this strategy to the benefit of the property owner, but friends and relatives of the owner are likely to view the virtual tour, and ultimately, to see your information as well.

Conclusion

Although I will attempt to convince you that advertising individual properties is not your best avenue to attract the most buyers, it is certainly something you must do in order to service your home sellers. Further, if you're planning to market a home online, be certain to do your best to attract the most buyers possible to view the online advertising.

Chapter 3 - Shifting Your Paradigm

The Cheese Moves

In the international best-selling book, *Who Moved My Cheese*, Spencer Johnson utilizes a short story about characters living in a maze to illustrate that things change and we have to adapt to those changes in order to succeed in life.[iv] Perhaps that's a grossly watered down explanation of the book, but it applies perfectly to so many of us in the real estate industry.

From around 2002 to 2006, buyers ran in our front door and begged us to buy homes before the prices got out of control. We became order takers, driving buyers to half a dozen homes to select one, writing quick offers and sending them off to a mortgage broker who would easily find them a low down payment, low interest loan. Some of us made very good livings without working all that hard.

At the end of 2006, the industry changed. The bubble burst. Credit became tighter. Mortgage programs evaporated and buyers

Loren Keim's Compelling Buyers to Call

stopped knocking on our doors. Five years later, there are some of you still sitting by the phone waiting for it to ring. Worse, some of you are sitting at home, not even bothering to come in the office anymore because there's no point.

In the book, *Who Moved My Cheese*, two of the characters effectively die waiting for the cheese to return. The other two find an incredible supply, but they had to work to find it.

We opened my firm back in the 1980's when interest rates were north of 15%, mortgage money was very difficult to find and buyers were even scarcer. This industry is a roller coaster, and although we go through periods of easy transactions, we also find ourselves just as often in market corrections, downturns, and every hundred years or so - a real estate depression. In the early 1980's, we had to create business for ourselves. Today, we have to do the same thing.

We all know the old line, "Insanity is doing the same thing over and over again but expecting different results." Yet, we do the same thing, day after day and year after year, hoping something will improve. You don't need to hope. You need to change.

What IS The Traditional Buyer Business?

We list a few homes for sale and then sit in the office praying for a buyer call. When someone actually *does* call us, we drop everything and drive halfway across the state to show them a house, only to find out they're not serious or they're not qualified to purchase. Worse, we've just trained those potential buyers that we will drop absolutely everything to run and meet them, which means from now on they'll be calling us at 10 pm and every weekend at the last minute to see homes.

Loren Keim's Compelling Buyers to Call

We kick ourselves for wasting our time, and yet we promise these unqualified buyers that probably aren't serious, that we'll set up a search on our MLS which will send them automatic emails of listings as they come on the market. Of course, the buyers that *are* serious are also getting automatic emails from a dozen other agents, too. We don't follow up with the buyers like we should. We never send a thank you note after meeting them and we forget to call them, relying on the automatic listing email to bring them back to us some day.

Am I depressing you, or am I being completely honest with you? Our business is completely unpredictable. Those buyers that we consider to be serious, we spend a week driving around, buying them lunch, and letting their kids spill stuff in the back of our leased car and we don't have any idea if they'll ever actually buy.

Let's face it. We have too many buyers that aren't qualified or aren't all that motivated, and we're feeling unhappy and stressed because we don't know if we're wasting our time, our energy and our gas. Some of us are thinking of giving up and getting a 'real job'.

The other part of this equation that we don't want to face is that the clients we work with can affect the way we, ourselves, feel and act. Our moods and our relationships with those closest to us can be negatively impacted by the stress we're experiencing. Realtors have one of the highest divorce rates of any profession. I firmly believe that although the divorce rate is partially due to the long hours we put into this profession and inconsistent income, it's more directly related to the fact that we bring our frustrations home to those we love.

On the other hand, if we're working with buyers that are well qualified, motivated to buy, and nice to us, that can affect us in a positive way. When I make a statement like that in a workshop, someone nearly always jumps up, aggravated that I could say such a thing, and says "Loren, if I could find qualified, motivated buyers who were ready to buy right now, I'd be working with them. All buyers are mean, rude people who only want to pay half the list price and will change their mind ten minutes before settlement."

"Ah," I might respond, "so you're only working with unqualified buyers who are not very serious because there's no alternative, right?"

I think we can all agree that there are a variety of potential buyers in any marketplace. One of our goals, aside from attracting them to contact us, is to separate and categorize them so we can spend our time in the most productive way possible, which means, spend time with those buyers who have the greatest motivation and are eminently qualified to purchase. Believe it or not, there are plenty of these potential buyers within miles of your office. Over the next few chapters, I'll show you how to entice them to raise their hands and identify themselves as potential buyers.

Many real estate speakers and trainers separate buyers into three categories: A, B and C. "A" buyers are those that are serious, qualified and have a moving date they have to meet. "B" buyers are those buyers who are serious and qualified but don't yet have a specific time frame in which they need to move, and "C" buyers are everybody else. Some real estate trainers actually tell you to completely ignore everybody else.

Loren Keim's Compelling Buyers to Call

I'd like to go a little deeper with our analysis of buyers, because ultimately I want you to build strong relationships and maximize the income you can earn from working with them.

1. **The Abuse-The-Realtor Buyer** - Buyers who don't take us seriously because we're salespeople. They have an expectation that we should be at their beck-and-call. Some of these buyers are serious, qualified and really want to purchase, but tend to abuse us. We can reduce our frustrations and create solid advocates of our personal real estate practice with this group *if* we take the time to properly educate them.

2. **Incubator Buyers:** Buyers want to buy, but they really aren't ready yet because they don't have the down payment, the closing costs, or they haven't yet corrected their credit. These are buyers we might incubate for a period of time.

3. **Fence-Sitter Buyers** - Clients who wish they could buy but don't believe they really can, or believe now is not the time to buy. Convincing these buyers that now *is* the time to buy often leads to referrals and to other potential buyers.

4. **Professional Lookers:** Professional lookers are customers who will probably never buy. They will use us, abuse us and waste our time driving them around to find the perfect home that doesn't actually exist in this plane of the universe.

5. **Bottom Feeders:** If they're buying homes to rent to others, we call them investors. If they are planning to live in a home and consistently offer 25% to 50% below asking price, they are bottom feeders. They will only buy if the price is far below market. Please don't misunderstand me. There's nothing wrong with wanting a good deal, but the likelihood of success with these

Loren Keim's Compelling Buyers to Call

buyers is close to zero.

6. **Anxious Buyer** – They want a home, and they really want it now. They are qualified and ready to purchase. You should probably live with these buyers until they purchase. The risk with these buyers is that they're so anxious; they may contact a dozen different Realtors in order to find the perfect home.

7. **Relocation Buyers** – Although some decide ultimately to rent and get to know the area, many are buyers who have the resources to purchase and a limited time to find the perfect home.

Obviously, the buyers you want to focus on most aggressively are those in the last two categories, the anxious buyer and the relocation buyer. Those agents who truly excel with buyers, however, look at the broader long-term picture. While many Realtors throw away the first three categories of buyers, because they're not ready to buy right this minute, these may ultimately be our best source of business over time.

Remember that if you can show someone the value of our service and that we truly care about them as individuals, not meal-tickets, they are likely to refer us customers forever. Successful agents know that during their careers the majority of their income will be referred to them by friends, relatives and those clients they assisted in buying or selling homes in the past. Those that refer the most clients tend to be the customers that we were able to connect with and to show that we truly care and do what's in the best interest of that client.

By all means, spend your time with the final two categories of buyers as often as possible, but be prepared to deal with all the other categories and have systems in place to help you succeed with them.

The Abuse-The-Realtor buyers need to be trained to work with you. That means making certain that you both set yourself apart as the

Loren Keim's Compelling Buyers to Call

expert in the field that they *have* to work with, which we'll be discussing in detail in Chapter 5. You'll also need to give a full buyer presentation, much like a listing presentation, to this type of buyer to insure success. A full buyer presentation outline is also included later in this book.

Incubator buyers may also be a steady source of referrals for the rest of your career, if you stick with them. Don't throw away buyers who are not ready to buy right now, but don't waste a lot of time showing them homes when they really can't purchase. Instead, plug them into a system of follow-up that will insure, when they're ready, that they come back to you because they can't possibly see themselves working with anyone else. This will be discussed in detail in the chapter on Follow-Up Systems.

Fence-Sitters are buyers we can often convert more quickly by providing them with the correct information, and showing them the benefits of purchasing a home now rather than waiting until next year. Again, a powerful follow-up system can be instrumental in converting these potential clients into purchasers and advocates of your personal real estate business.

Regardless of the type of buyer we attract, our initial goal is to create a system that generates a steady stream of buyers who are qualified to buy and are either motivated or can be motivated. What would it do to your business if you had a lead generation system that produced multiple opportunities regularly so you could select which buyers were the best to work with?

Even better, what if you could differentiate yourself from the competitors so clients would *want* to work with you and work by *your* schedule?

Loren Keim's Compelling Buyers to Call

Honestly, Why Do We Advertise?

After the first ninety minutes of any of my workshops, we take a break and I invariably have a handful of Realtors who come to the front, frustrated that I haven't yet given them "the ad" to run that will magically make buyers appear. Again, we need to change your whole philosophy about attracting customers or too many of you won't understand why we're looking at advertising and marketing techniques that are so alien to the way you've conducted your business since you were first licensed.

Why *do* we advertise? Do we advertise to attract a buyer for the property we're advertising? Do you really believe if you run an ad on a particular property that a buyer will come forward and buy the home? Do we advertise to appease the home seller? Or do we really advertise in order to identify someone thinking of buying now or in the near future?

It doesn't matter if you're advertising in the local newspaper, in a real estate magazine, on television or on Facebook or Google. Your goal is exactly the same – to identify someone who wants to buy or sell real estate, and then to entice that person to work with *you* instead of Bill over at Doggie-Breath Realty. Whether we want to admit it or not, that's how you make a living and that's how we've all made a living for the last hundred years or so, which is about how long Bill from Doggie-Breath has been in the business.

Ten years ago, when a buyer called on a property from the newspaper, we all *knew* that person would never buy the home they called on. Why? Because the odds are against it. Buyers looked through newspapers and home magazines, circling dozens of homes, trying to narrow down their search to two or three homes that they'd actually *look at* and then hopefully make an offer on one. Of course, this isn't the way the real world works, but buyers were calling us from newspapers to

Loren Keim's Compelling Buyers to Call

determine which homes to eliminate from their list, so they could narrow that list down.

Skilled Realtors and brokers were able to 'switch' buyers from one property to others. "Oh, that home is not the school district you're looking for? Well, what school district ARE you considering?"

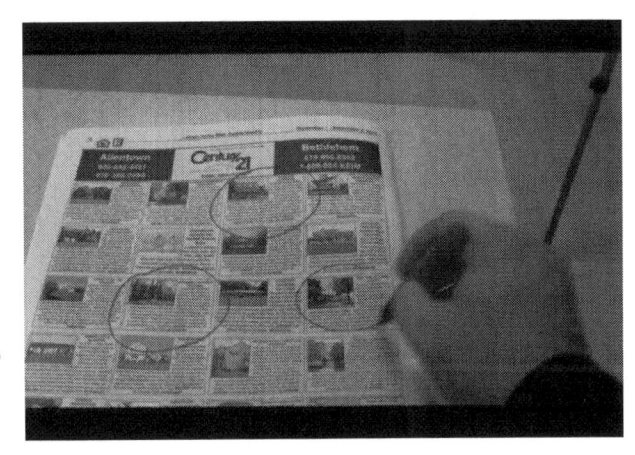

"Really? There are lots of homes in that district that might meet your needs. Hold on, I'm pulling up some on the computer. The house you called about was $350,000. Are you looking in that general price range?"

The difference between the average agent who lasts in the industry for eleven months and those who last in the industry for a lifetime, making an above average income, is directly proportional to their skill at converting clients.

I can't begin to estimate how many times I've heard an agent say "I'm sorry – that home is sold. Is there anything else I can help you with? No? Okay, thanks. Good bye." By the way, that print media ad call just cost your office $117, and you blew it. Someone called the office and identified themselves as a customer considering purchasing a home and you told them that a *particular* home was sold and then let them go without ever asking what they wanted, when they were planning to buy or even what their name was. And by the way, helping that client to find

Loren Keim's Compelling Buyers to Call

the perfect home is not just to benefit you – it's in the client's best interests as well to find a good Realtor who will help them find the perfect home.

That client will call ten or fifteen or twenty Realtors until they find one who helps them, and becomes their buyer's agent. We all know, from National Association studies, that between three and six of every ten callers will eventually purchase a home from someone. Do you want that someone to be you or your competitor? Which of you will take care of that client and do what's in the client's best interest, helping them to make the best possible decisions?

The primary difference between ten or twenty years ago and today is that most buyers are no longer calling us from newspapers or magazines. They're calling us from our online advertising. The internet is a strong marketing arm for our businesses when it's utilized correctly.

Regardless of what type of client you're seeking, there are four keys to prospecting to find clients. First you need to figure out who you're going to direct your message to. Who is your target market? In this program, obviously our focus is prospecting to identify likely home buyers.

Second, you're going to have to select your method of contact. Although we'll use a variety of methods, our focus will include the Internet, Websites and Social Media as a primary contact method.

Loren Keim's Compelling Buyers to Call

The third component is the key to real success with your campaigns. Simply posting, emailing or advertising isn't enough. We have to find a way to entice potential clients to identify themselves as possibly considering buying or selling. You have to create a burning need for potential customers to respond to your message. You can do this by positioning yourself differently than the typical Realtor, utilizing a unique selling proposition, or by giving your prospect something of value.

Finally, you have to have a solid method of follow-up in place so you can build a relationship with each potential customer who contacts you.

In the long run, you'll also deliver exceptional service which will net you those coveted referrals that grow your individual real estate business. You'll also stay in contact after the sale, which will lead to even more referrals. Before you can deliver that exceptional service and build those relationships, however, you have to find clients.

Although I mentioned the significant impact of the Internet on our business, please remember that the internet is a tool. It is a tool to prospect for clients, to keep in touch with clients, to deliver information and to help build long-term relationships. It is still a tool, however, just a lot more powerful than a home magazine and a telephone.

The Internet is a Tool
- To Prospect for Clients
- To Keep in Touch with Clients
- To Deliver Information
- To Help Build Relationships

Loren Keim's Compelling Buyers to Call

Why Doesn't Most Advertising Work?

Realtors primarily run two kinds of ads, either advertising themselves, known as image advertising, or advertising specific homes. Neither of these forms of advertising is particularly effective in reaching the maximum possible number of buyers.

Image Advertising

Image advertising certainly feed our egos. Society, particularly in America, has moved in the direction of 'me first.' One only has to look at the inane things that are written on Facebook and Twitter, such as 'just went to the bathroom' and 'going to bed' to see how self-focused many of us have become. But honestly, does image advertising attract clients to contact us?

Don't misunderstand me, I have done my fair share of image advertising, personal promotion and marketing campaigns over my career. For example, like many other agents, I sent out a postcard with the words *"Loren Keim is outstanding in his field."* The postcard featured a photo of me standing in the middle of a field. There are people who can recall some of my more creative postcards and messages years after I send them.

Unfortunately, that doesn't give the prospect the desire to pick up the phone and call me; it simply builds an image in their mind. For a campaign to be truly successful, there needs to be a direct tie between the advertising and some action that you want a prospect to take.

Loren Keim's Compelling Buyers to Call

Stop Running Image Ads

Got Realtor®?
Wanda Wallabee
BestRealtorEver.com

    Before someone writes me nasty letters about the number of clients they've attracted simply by putting their face on some billboards, let me explain that in the long-term, you may build yourself into a brand. Attendees at my workshops will say "People that I've never met send me referrals because they know my name" or "Customers feel like they know me before they even meet me." Every so often I picked up a client from name reputation as well, but I probably spent ten thousand dollars in image advertising for every one client I found through it. Was that money well spent?

    Over time, a series of *any* type of marketing can brand you as an expert and create name recognition, but again, does someone knowing your name really lead to many people calling you? How much do you have to spend to build that solid name reputation? When someone decides to buy a home, will they call you from your billboard and newsletter or will they call the person who has a sign in front of the home they like? If they're nervous, will they call someone from image advertising, or will they be more likely to work with the Realtor referred to them by their cousin Jennifer?

Loren Keim's Compelling Buyers to Call

Individual Property Advertising

We might as well admit that we all waste money on advertising our listings because we want to appease our home sellers and deep down, we hope someone calls from the ad and buys the house. The truth, however, is that if the house doesn't sell, the sellers still aren't happy. They will blame you and your poor advertising despite the fact that you spent more money on the home than any other Realtor would have, right?

Most home advertisements look the same. They tell potential clients the style of the home, the number of bedrooms and baths, the school district and the price. How often do buyers *actually* buy the home they call about? More often than not, the buyer finds a reason to cross the home off their list and attempts to hang up on you.

After thirty seconds on the phone with you, the buyer determines that the home is in the wrong neighborhood, or the taxes are too high or the yard is too big or too small. Successful Realtors are able to switch some of these calls into buyers by keeping them talking and determining their wants and needs.

There is a better way. When you run a specific individual property ad, you're actually limiting the buyers who might call you. I'll prove that in a few paragraphs.

In his book *You Squared*, Price Pritchett writes, "*It's just past noon, late July and I'm listening to the desperate sounds of a life or death struggle going on a few feet away.*"[v] He's in a hotel room in Toronto watching a fly bang its head into a window over and over again, trying to escape the room, while an open door stands only a few feet away.

Loren Keim's Compelling Buyers to Call

In the real estate industry, we play follow-the-leader, with all of us running the same kinds of ads, garnering the same kinds of results and all pretending that we're going to somehow do better than our competitors.

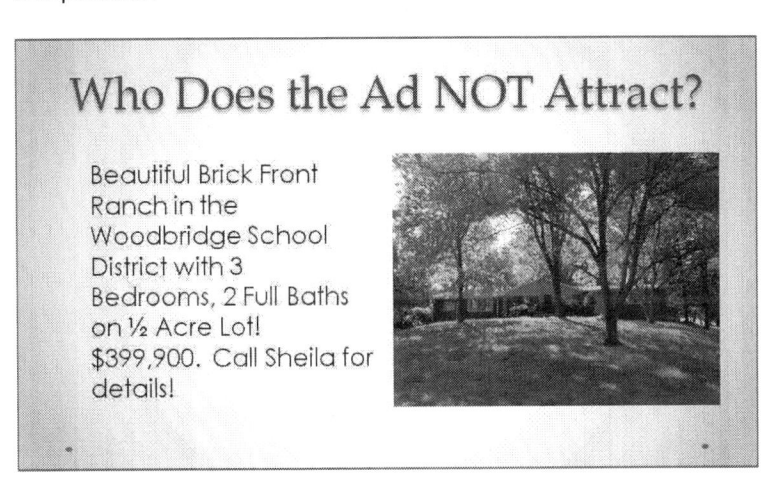

Who Does the Ad NOT Attract?

Beautiful Brick Front Ranch in the Woodbridge School District with 3 Bedrooms, 2 Full Baths on ½ Acre Lot! $399,900. Call Sheila for details!

Who is attracted to an advertisement for a house like the one pictured above? The person who is attracted is that person who really wants a one story home in the Woodbridge School District on half an acre. Remember that our goal in advertising or marketing is not *just* to sell this particular house, but rather to identify someone who is thinking about buying a home now and get them to raise their hand and identify themselves as a buyer. This ad attracts one subset of potential buyers in the market.

Who is *not* attracted to the ad? Someone who absolutely wants two stories won't be attracted. If a buyer is willing to accept three bedrooms, and really wants the Woodbridge School District, but wants two stories, they will not ever call on this advertisement. Someone who wants a ranch in the area, but doesn't want a half acre of grass to cut also won't call.

Loren Keim's Compelling Buyers to Call

In fact, unless the buyer wants, or is willing to accept, the type of home, location, number of bedrooms, number of baths, lot size and price range of this home, they will not ever call. So how many potential buyers looked at this advertisement and did not call you? Our goal is to identify as many of them as possible, and this ad is limiting us to *only* those that have interest in all the characteristics we outline in our ad copy.

Switching

Although I've mentioned repeatedly that advertising specific homes is one of the least successful methods of attracting buyers, you still need to excel at handling incoming calls in order to grow your business. The phone is the lifeblood of our industry. Whether we are making prospecting calls to obtain listing appointments, negotiating sales contracts or handling incoming buyer calls, we must make an effort to make every phone call count. Keep in mind that a single advertisement on your listing may cost a hundred dollars or more. That advertisement may only generate a call or two, so your skill at converting those calls to prospects can create a huge return on your advertising investment, or place a drain on your savings.

As I will repeat continually throughout this text, our goal with most advertising is to get prospective buyers to raise their hands and say "Hey, I'm out here looking for a property". Once we identify a potential buyer, we can start directing our efforts to get them to work with us. Eventually, we'll have to find a way to meet with the client, qualify them, introduce them to the concept of buyer's agency and show them properties. First, we have to get over the initial objection that they don't want to see the property they are calling us about.

One method of accomplishing this task is by switching the caller to other properties that might be a better fit for the client. When you are

Loren Keim's Compelling Buyers to Call

advertising a property for sale, it pays to know the properties that are most likely competing with yours. Schedule some time to preview competing properties so that you have a clear picture of what else is available in the marketplace. Then, as callers ask about your property, you can intersperse questions about what would be the caller's perfect property, and lead into other properties on the market.

Caller: "Where is the advertised property located?"

Agent: "I'm just pulling up the details on that on my computer. I'll have it in a second. What area are you considering?"

Caller: "I'd like to stay in mid-Bucks County , preferably Doylestown or Perkasie, but I'd really like to be close to Route 309 for commuting to my job."

Agent: "Route 309? How much were you looking to spend?"

Caller: "I'm not exactly sure. I don't want to be paying more than $2500 a month."

Agent: "That's fine. I have that property in front of me now. It's actually located close to Lansdale . Would that area work for you?"

Caller: "No, I'm sorry. That's too far for me."

Agent: "No problem. You mentioned you wanted to be close to Route 309. I remember a similar property that was for sale in that area. It's a really sharp looking brick ranch, but it may be a bit higher in price than you'd like to go. Can I look that one up for you and call you back with the information?"

Caller: "Sure."

Agent: "Great. What's your phone number?"

Loren Keim's Compelling Buyers to Call

Remember that one of your primary goals in the initial phone call is to obtain the client's name, phone number, and most importantly, their permission to call them back with more information.

When any client calls, keep three important notes in the back of your mind. First, two out of every three callers is going to buy a home this year. They'll buy from you or from someone down the street at Sticky Fingers Realty. Buyers are also people just like you, and they really need your help.

Second, they will not buy the home they're calling about. Sorry, but that's the truth. Finally, they are almost never calling about one home. In a magazine, they have circled a dozen. If they're driving through a neighborhood, they wrote down the phone numbers of other homes for sale as well. If they're online, they've found a dozen to ask about.

One other piece of advice on handling calls comes from a trainer I learned from early in my career. Smile when you speak to someone on the phone. Although they can't see you when you answer the phone, the smile naturally relaxes you and shines through in your manner and speech. That trainer actually put mirrors on each agent's phone so they'd focus on maintaining that smile.

You will primarily receive three types of incoming calls about specific properties: sign calls, print ad calls and Internet ad calls.

Sign Calls

Property for-sale signs are one of the best sources of buyer leads. My non-scientific study of these sign calls leads me to the conclusion that the house is more than the caller can afford to purchase. More often than not, the house is beyond the buyer's means.

Loren Keim's Compelling Buyers to Call

They obviously already know and like the location of the property, so the likely objections are either the asking price or the size of the home. In either case, your goal is to find out what price range the caller is comfortable with, or what size the caller requires.

I imagine a husband and wife, out on a Sunday drive, passing by a few homes they have interest in. One spouse says to the other "Look, honey, it's perfect." The other replies, "We can't afford it." The first responds, "We won't know until we call and ask, will we?"

Caller: "Hi, I'm calling about the house on the corner of 5th and Broad, what is the asking price?"

Agent: "Let me pull up the details on that property on my computer. I'll have it in a second. That's a two story colonial, right? Is that the type of home you're looking to buy?"

Caller: "Yes, I'd prefer two stories."

Agent: "Ok. Is that the general location you'd like?"

Caller: "I'd like to stay in the Parkland School District, but still remain close to I-78."

Agent: "I have that property on my screen now. They're currently asking $325,000. How much were you looking to spend?"

Caller: "Wow. That's high. I'm not looking for anything over $250,000."

Agent: "No problem. You said you were looking for a two story home and wanted to stay in Parkland. How many bedrooms and baths do you need?"

Caller: "Well, I need at least 4 bedrooms and 2 full baths."

Loren Keim's Compelling Buyers to Call

Agent: "Okay. I remember a similar property that was for sale in the area. I don't think it had a sign on it, because the owner didn't want anyone to know he's selling. Can I look that one up for you and call you back with the information?"

Caller: "That would be fine."

Agent: "Great. What's your phone number?"

An alternate approach to sign calls is to try to determine if the caller has written down several properties. Buyers looking for properties tend to drive through areas, and may write down the agency names and numbers on several properties for sale. Rather than allow the prospect to call several other agents, who may pick them up as a potential client, you can research the same information for them.

Agent: "While you were driving around, did you see any other properties that interested you? They don't have to be listed by my firm."

Client: "I noticed a few."

Agent: "That's great. I can actually look them up for you now in our database. I can pull up all the information and let you know those prices as well. It's a bit easier than you calling through different agencies for information."

Caller: "I didn't realize you could do that."

Agent: "Definitely. Actually, we have a great software program at our company as well that helps us to find the perfect property. Each morning, the program searches all the new properties that came on the market by every agency in the system. It then emails you a copy of each of the new listings as they come on the market. This way, you know about properties before they are ever advertised. Often, the best listings sell quickly, sometimes before a sign is even put in the yard."

Caller: "That sounds great."

Agent: "Well, let me pull up information on the other properties you drove by, and then we'll talk about your needs and try to get you into our Automatic Property Search program."

Incidentally, most agents have access to automatic search programs. Different MLS systems offer the service. What differentiates you from the competition is that you're using it as a tool to convince buyers and tenants to work with you.

Newspaper and Magazine Advertisement Calls

Prospective clients researching properties for sale in the newspaper or in home magazines seldom know the exact address or location of the property being advertised. As Realtors, we omit the address in order to generate a call. The number one reason a buyer eliminates an advertised property from their list is that the specific location isn't what the buyer wants.

As with sign calls, these callers are probably not just considering one advertisement in the periodical. The likelihood is that they have circled several in the same newspaper or magazine. You can again ask them if they'd have interest in you pulling information on any other properties they may have circled.

Caller: "Where is the advertised property located?"

Agent: "I'm just pulling up the details on that on my computer. I'll have it in a second. What area are you considering?"

Loren Keim's Compelling Buyers to Call

Caller: "I'd like to be close to the shore points. I'm particularly interested in property south of the turnpike."

Agent: "The shore points? That's my favorite area. How much were you looking to spend?"

Caller: "Probably no more than a half million, unless it's a truly spectacular property."

Agent: "That's fine. I have that property in front of me now. It's actually located in Tapani, pretty far inland. I'm guessing that area wouldn't work for you?"

Caller: "No, I'm sorry. That's not where I'm looking to buy."

Agent: "You said you pulled this advertisement from the Morning News?"

Caller: "Yes."

Agent: "While you were looking through the ads, did any others stand out that might interest you? They don't have to be listed by my firm."

Client: "About 5 or 6."

Agent: "That's great. I can actually look them up for you now in our database. I can pull up all the information and let you know those prices as well. It's a bit easier than you calling through different agencies for information."

Caller: "Really?"

Agent: "Definitely. Actually, we have a great software program at our company as well that helps us to find the perfect property. Each morning, the program searches all the new properties that came on the market by every agency in the system. It then emails you a copy of each of the new listings as they come on the market. This way, you know about properties before they're ever advertised. The best listings sell quickly, often before a sign goes up or the first ad is run."

Caller: "That sounds great."

Agent: "Well, let me pull up information on the other properties you drove by, and then we'll talk about your needs and try to get you into our Automatic Property Search program."

Internet Calls

Prospects calling from Internet advertising are generally more interested in the property than the typical sign call or newspaper ad call because they usually have more information about the property. Most real estate sites on the Internet will display the general location of the property, the price, the size of the home, and the number of bedrooms and bath.

Again, whether they set up an appointment to see the home they call about or not, they have pulled up several homes on the Internet from several different brokers. Ask them what other homes they've selected and set up an appointment to show them all the homes.

Summary

Although we know that our advertising is not effective, we continue to spend more each year trying to attract that small percentage of potential clients who will respond. The two most popular forms of marketing for Realtors are individual property ads and agent image ads. We run property ads and image ads because we do what everyone else is doing, rather than innovating better attraction techniques. There *are* better methods of attracting customers.

Chapter 4 - Compelling Offers and Free Information

In the last chapter, I tried to build a case for doing something different than all your competitors. Stop simply running individual property ads and ego boosting image ads. Let's look at marketing concepts that might be a bit outside your comfort zone.

What Are Compelling Offers?

There is a much better way to attract clients and entice them to raise their hands and let you know they're in the market to buy or sell. That method is by offering the customer something of value, or a fair trade that lowers the barrier of resistance a client has for calling you.

Something of value may be a free report or guide that will help their specific situation. It may be an offer of an over-the-phone evaluation of their property or the property they'd like to buy, or a special tool such as an automatic listing update program.

Loren Keim's Compelling Buyers to Call

Making an offer of a free report or free information is not only a broad means of appealing to a larger audience, but has the added benefit that you don't need to personally have any listings to entice buyers to contact you with this method.

This technique, originally introduced to me by real estate trainer Gerry Ballinger, is known as Direct Response Marketing. Since meeting Gerry, I've seen very similar materials from great trainers like Joe Stumpf[vi], Terry Hunefeld, Jay Abraham, and Craig Proctor. Each uses a "direct response" mechanism in their marketing to get clients to identify themselves *as* clients or to lower the barrier of resistance in speaking with you.

In many cases, top trainers like these suggest that you create advertisements that look like news articles. Consumers don't like "*sales people*" trying to "*sell them*" something. When they see advertisements that are sales-like, they put up their defenses. The potential customer believes that something must be untrue or hidden in the advertisement. In fact, many consumers will actively avoid speaking with an agent who uses the phrase "*Be Sold On ...*" because they believe they themselves will be *sold*.

Everyone likes to buy, but no one likes to be sold. So if buyers aren't directly attracted by advertising, what *does* pique the interest of potential customers?

Part of your brain helps you to focus on those things that are most important to you at any point in time. This part of the brain is called your reticular activator. Have you ever noticed when you buy a new car that you're proud of, you start noticing that exact same car everywhere? It seems like everyone just ran out and bought one. You're noticing other cars like yours because you're tuned into them with your reticular activator.

Loren Keim's Compelling Buyers to Call

Pregnant women seem to notice other pregnant women. Baseball fans notice baseball memorabilia and those interested in Nascar seem to find Nascar everywhere.

Likewise, those who would like to purchase a home, whether they are first time buyers or move-up buyers, are tuned in to the real estate market, and they are more likely to notice for sale signs, real estate related articles, news stories relating to real estate and so on. We can use the reticular activator to identify potential buyers by enticing them to see our messages. Later in this book, I'll outline how to use this technique to train your buyers to find other buyers for you with their reticular activators.

This technique of creating articles that give away free information to the consumer allows the agent to fly under the radar of the consumer's defense mechanism. If consumers can view you as a valuable partner in the process of buying or selling, rather than a salesperson running an ad, you are ninety percent of the way to extraordinary success in your chosen field.

Unfortunately, this technique is far outside the scope of how most real estate agents and brokers think. In fact, many Realtors will actively argue with me when I teach it. *"No one is going to call for some pamphlet. If we want buyers, we need to advertise homes."* I can tell you from experience that I have received significantly more calls on correctly structured newsworthy ads than I have from any advertisement on a particular home because all potential buyers may respond to a newsworthy call to action to deliver free information on the buying process while not all buyers will respond to any individual ad on a particular home.

As I write about these techniques, please don't misunderstand, there are places and times for image advertising. For many years, I've used sign riders that read *"Keim Sold Mine!"* When you are trying to actively build name recognition, cute ads may get you noticed, but they do not give a potential buyer a powerful reason to contact you right now.

Attraction Techniques

Understanding how to attract prospective buyers, sellers and investors to call you is both a science and an art form. You must start by considering what the prospective client desires and needs, and just as important, what they will actively avoid. Think from their perspective.

For example, in most cases, buyers do not really want to talk to us. They are afraid of being sold, or of someone trying to talk them into a decision that they are not prepared to make. What they really want is information.

When you buy a car, you certainly want to know what the best deals are, what the best vehicles are, how each car handles when you drive and so forth. You probably do *not,* however, want some slick car salesperson coming up to talk to you about *"this little baby"* that he can get you a great deal on, right? That's exactly how most buyers feel when they're considering purchasing a home. Even if you're the most professional Realtor this side of Mars, you're still considered a salesperson by much of the public.

Think of their needs and desires first. Next, try to put those needs and desires into a strong headline that will tempt the customer into reading the rest of the article or advertisement. Have you ever noticed how many people read the headlines in tabloids at the grocery store checkout? The headlines capture enough attention that a certain percentage of the public buys the tabloid and reads the articles, even though they realize the article is probably fictitious garbage.

Loren Keim's Compelling Buyers to Call

How do we use the same technique in a newsworthy headline to attract potential buyers? *"Local Couple mauled by Lion while viewing new home at Open House"* or *"Local home, haunted by Victoria Secret Model, will be open this weekend"* would probably cause a potential client to read the article, but certainly would not fit the category of filling their needs or desires.

The three primary messages that capture attention are an opportunity for gain, a fear of loss or a strong curiosity about a subject. By far, a fear of loss is the most powerful. Strong headlines that target specific potential buyers might include:

- **The 17 deadly mistakes Home Buyers make when buying their first home** – this headline is based on a fear of loss. Buyers don't want to make mistakes when purchasing a home. Many decide they *need* to know what those mistakes are.

- **How to avoid common mistakes that cost home buyers thousands of dollars.** A variation of the prior headline. Test each and see which pulls the greatest number of potential buyers, or create your own.

- **New report reveals the secrets to buying a home with little or no money down.** This headline appeals to a buyer's curious nature and also is an opportunity to gain. We've actually had buyers purchase a home with cash that responded to a "no money down" report. They're still tuned into buying property and *need* to know how someone can buy with no money down.

- **Learn the secrets of buying foreclosure homes with new report.** This report is based on the opportunity for gain. Buyers assume that foreclosure homes are the 'best deals' and want information on how to beat other buyers to those great deals.

- **Beat Other Buyers to the Hottest Foreclosure Listings.** A variation of the prior headline.

Loren Keim's Compelling Buyers to Call

- **Don't spend one more dime on rent until you read this new free report by industry insiders.**

Rather than taking a broad approach to marketing for buyers, you may try to zero in on likely buyer groups. Although this limits the potential pool of respondents, it may resonate more quickly with them.

For Specific Groups:

- <u>Move-Up Buyers</u> – The secrets to moving up to a bigger home at the lowest possible cost.

- <u>Seniors</u> - Free report reveals methods to keep your money when moving to senior housing.

- <u>Buying a Farm?</u> - New report reveals the deadliest mistakes made by farm buyers that cost them tens of thousands of dollars.

- <u>Investors</u> – The truth about property flipping is revealed in a new free report.

- <u>Investors</u> – Special tax program allows investors to buy and sell property and pay no capital gains!

The same approach can be utilized to attract home sellers:

Sellers:

- The secrets to selling your home in a slow market. This can be viewed as a fear of loss or an opportunity for gain.

- Local agent reveals guerrilla tactics for marketing homes.

- New home seller report helps local couple save thousands when selling home.

Loren Keim's Compelling Buyers to Call

- ❑ Don't sell your home until you learn the 19 critical errors made by homeowners selling for top dollar.

- ❑ Learn 25 inexpensive repairs that could increase the value of your home with our new report.

Newsworthy Marketing

In addition to creating a headline that catches the potential buyer's attention, you should carefully focus your message on the emotional hot buttons of the likely audience you're trying to attract. What pain are they trying to avoid? What benefit will entice them to read further?

Once you have selected who may be your target audience for your message, determined their needs, and crafted a headline to address those needs, you'll need to build the body of the article. The article should continue to build on the potential customers emotions. Why do they want to move? What is the most likely pain that drives them to look for a home? Is it the cramped space of their current home or their apartment? What are their needs and their ultimate hopes and dreams for a better lifestyle?

**New Government Program Helps
Allentown Buyer Purchase Home with
No Money Down.**

Allentown, PA - Carmen looked back at the steep steps leading up to her old apartment for the last time as she loaded her car with the last of her personal belongings. Carmen had spent 3 long years in the cramped apartment with her husband and daughter, Ashley. Recently, she discovered a new government loan program...

Loren Keim's Compelling Buyers to Call

The entire article is scripted to show the potential home buyer that they really *can* do what they want to do, if only they had a little more information, which you can provide them at absolutely no charge. Remember that buyers buy emotionally, and sellers sell emotionally. Logic, unfortunately, often plays a very small role in moving.

A tenant wants to get out of the endless loop of throwing money away in rent. This future home buyer wants something to call their own, to build equity, to have a yard for their children, and to paint the colors they want to paint. Draw each of these into your story as you write it.

> *"Tears welled in Carmen's eyes as she considered the years that she spent trying to save enough money to buy a home of her own. At one point she thought it would never happen because the bills always seemed to be greater than her income."*

These articles can be used in dozens of different media. An advertisement that looks like an article can be run in the local newspaper, local homes magazine or any periodical. These stories can be turned into postcards and mailed to your target groups. An article like the example above may be mailed to renters in apartment complexes, or perhaps even photocopied and slipped under the door.

We've successfully used newsworthy articles in newsletters, postcards and even on the on our websites. Each story is geared to the target group, speaking emotionally to that group and their needs. Each story also offers free information to help the group accomplish the same end result as those in the story.

Free Reports

ERA Real Estate ran a successful advertising campaign several

Loren Keim's Compelling Buyers to Call

years ago offering a free book or guide on how to purchase a home. Certainly, they received many calls from people who simply wanted the free book. However, the campaign allowed ERA to compile a list of potential clients who responded to their advertising, thereby allowing the company to begin a more targeted campaign of connecting with *those* particular clients, rather than using the shotgun approach to marketing.

Most of us can't afford to publish a book and send free copies all over creation for anyone who calls in, so we have to find a more cost effective method of achieving the same results.

How to Buy Your First Home
The First Time Home Buyer Handbook!

A simple solution is to create trifold pamphlets or short three to five page booklets that succinctly answer the question advertised in the article.

Unfortunately, this is where I tend to lose most agents unless I provide them with copies of these informational pamphlets. The task of actually writing a thousand word pamphlet or guide seems to be too daunting for most agents. The truth, however, is that it is relatively easy to write a short guide and it is good practice to determine what really *is* beneficial to a potential client.

For example, you may advertise that home buyers make many mistakes that cost them thousands of dollars when buying a home. That is a true statement. Buyers hire the wrong mortgage company and are charged "junk fees." Buyers neglect to have home inspections because they want to save that money, but end up with significant problems that may cost significantly more than any inspection. Buyers don't research the area, neighborhood or schools properly when initially purchasing, and so on.

Can you take a few minutes and write down the mistakes you've seen buyers or sellers make? Can you have lunch with a few other agents and share ideas of what mistakes buyers and sellers make?

Take the list, number the mistakes one through whatever, and write a short description of what each mistake means, why it costs home buyers money and how to avoid the mistake. Tada! You have a free report that you can advertise.

You can write a short list with a paragraph about each, as I've started below, or you can write out an entire page of information about each mistake.

The Costliest Mistakes Made by Home Buyers and How to Avoid Them.

Mistake #1 - Hiring the Wrong Mortgage Company

Shopping for the perfect mortgage? Are you comparing companies in the newspaper and online for their interest rates? Some mortgage companies appear to guarantee buyers the lowest interest rates, but if the buyer isn't careful, these mortgage companies may make

Loren Keim's Compelling Buyers to Call

up the difference in payment by charging huge processing fees that are referred to in the industry as junk fees. Far too often, home buyers discover that a good deal isn't always what it seems.

Some online mortgage companies have been found to provide incorrect closing costs because they're out-of-state and unfamiliar with localized closing costs such as transfer taxes. Worse, there are mortgage companies that charge an application fee on a credit card and then fail to deliver a mortgage on time for your closing.

Ask friends, relatives and your Realtor which mortgage companies have consistently provided good service. My team at *Awesomely Cool Real Estate* can provide you with a list of mortgage companies we've worked with locally. Call us at 610-555-8000 for a no obligation list.

Mistake #2 - Neglecting to Have a Home Inspection

Would you buy an old used car without having it thoroughly inspected by someone you know and trust? A home may have issues which will cost far more than any car repair, and purchasing a home may be the most expensive investment you make in your lifetime.

Any home may have hidden defects that could cost thousands of dollars to repair. A failing septic system may cost an owner tens of thousands of dollars. Mold problems may create health issues for you or your children. Radon gas may cause cancer. Lead paint, water penetration and hundreds of other issues may be avoided when they are discovered by a home inspector before you buy the home.

Spending a few hundred dollars to investigate potential defects or expensive repairs in a home could literally save you many thousands in the long run. If you're planning to purchase a home and would like a free list of professional, licensed home inspectors, call our team at *Awesomely*

Loren Keim's Compelling Buyers to Call

Cool Real Estate.

Mistake #3 - Not Doing the Proper Research

Double check the property taxes, the school district, the neighborhood, your commuting distance to work and anything else that may affect your enjoyment of the home you're about to purchase. Choosing the wrong home, or purchasing too quickly without proper research, can lead to headache and heartache after the sale.

Mistake #4 - Not Hiring a Buyer's Agent

Do you realize that buyer representation is free with firms like *Awesomely Cool Real Estate*? You get professional, personal representation in the purchase of a home without paying a dime.

Why is that important? Why can't you simply call the listing agent for each property you might want to view? Many home buyers don't realize that the listing agent for the property is likely to represent the best interests of the home seller, not you. That means their fiduciary responsibility is to the seller. They have to disclose everything you tell them and they have an obligation to get you to pay the highest price possible for the home.

A buyer's agent represents *your* interests instead of the sellers, and you don't pay anything for that service.

Mistake #5 – Working with Several Realtors at the Same Time

Some homebuyers feel that if they simply talk to many agents, there will be that many more Realtors out in the market trying to find the best home. The truth is usually the opposite...

Loren Keim's Compelling Buyers to Call

While the text of the mistakes above are a quickly written example, you can certainly put together a list of common mistakes made by home buyers, by home sellers, by investors or nearly any group and build reports that you can advertise.

Gooder Group

For those of you who are still outright terrified of writing reports, go to www.GooderGroup.com. The Gooder Group has written many different full-color brochures for Realtors and mortgage professionals and makes these title available for a fee.

Some of the Gooder Group's current informational booklets include:

- ❏ REO: What Every Buyer Needs to Know to Purchase a Foreclosed Property.
- ❏ BARGAINS: 9 Sure-Fire Ways to Find Bargain Properties Today.

Loren Keim's Compelling Buyers to Call

- BUYER'S MARKET: How To Take Advantage of a Buyer's Market.

- NEW HOMES: 10 Secrets You Should Know Before You Visit Your First Model Home

- PRE-INSPECT: How To Inspect A Home Before You Make An Offer

- POINTS: Sharp Ways To Make Mortgage Points Work For You

- RENT vs BUY: How To Make The Best Use Of Your Housing Dollars

- RENTALS: 7 Secrets You Must Know To Succeed As A Landlord

- SECOND HOMES: Why Now Is The Time To Buy

- SECRETS: Nine Deadly Traps To Avoid When Buying A Home

- SMART BUYING: 8 Inside Tips Every Buyer Must Know In Today's Market

- MAKEOVERS: 20 Low-Cost Ways To Drive Up Your Home's Value

and many more.

Free Reports on the Internet

Web sites are really marketing, advertising and informational vehicles. Those of you who have a web site set up that simply states: "Rebecca Sells Denver Homes", and has glamour shots of you, need to re-think your online strategy.

Loren Keim's Compelling Buyers to Call

[Screenshot of a website with banners reading "Rebecca Sells Denver Homes!", "Simply the Best! I Sell Every Kind of Home", and "Rebecca Sells Denver — Thinking of Selling? Call Rebecca First!!"]

Again, no one will call Rebecca to buy or sell a home from a simple ad saying "Rebecca sells Denver homes", and if they do, I would question their motives. When you add your properties for sale to a site, you pick up a little bit of response. You typically won't get a tremendous response because most buyers know they can go directly to Realtor.com, the local multiple listing site or another large site and find everyone's listings.

A method to attract the customers viewing your website to contact you is by offering something of value. A banner on your site for home sellers, who will become move-up buyers, may offer, *"Learn 25 inexpensive repairs that could increase the value of your home with our new report."* A banner to attract buyers might be "*New Free Report Reveals the Truth About Whether Foreclosures are the Best Buys!*"

There are two keys to making this work. First, give enough information that the client *has to have* a copy of the report. Second, don't give it to them without getting their information. They need to fill out an online form in order to receive their copy of the report.

Loren Keim's Compelling Buyers to Call

This information is critical because part of the process of prospecting for buyers is to identify them so you can set up a system to regularly contact those clients.

Any online form should include contact information, such as name, address, phone number and email address. The form should also allow the user to fill out a form on what they would like to purchase or sell, and ask for the time frame of their considered move.

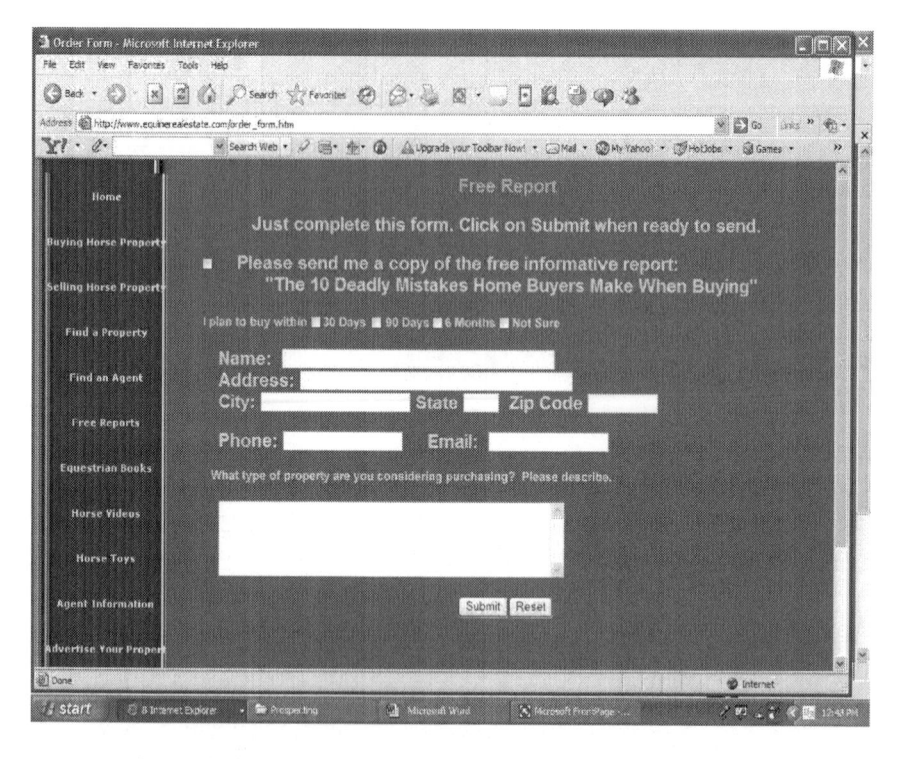

I do not believe it's necessary to ask the user to fill out some huge form with lots of information because you're more likely to cause the user to simply give up and close the window. The less information you can ask for while still learning about the prospect, the more likely you are to get them to fill out the form.

Loren Keim's Compelling Buyers to Call

Market Evaluations

Offering free information or something of value to a client may include a no-cost or no obligation market evaluation of their property, or an estimate of what homes are selling for in particular neighborhoods. While this text is about prospecting for buyers, remember that having listings generates buyers and many home sellers become buyers when their homes sell. Buyers use similar tools, such as Zillow, in order to determine price ranges of homes.

Remember that you are trying to lower the barrier of resistance for a client to contact you and identify themselves as a potential customer of your business. The prospect really doesn't want you coming over to their home because they believe you'll try to sell them on yourself and listing the property. Likewise, the buyer doesn't want you meeting with them simply to give them an idea of what homes are selling for.

The harder you try to get in the door to meet with them, the more likely they are to believe you are a pushy salesperson. However, the person who *does* get in the home seller's door first is the most likely person to eventually get the listing and works to find them their new home, so you don't simply want to continually send information.

Giving away information helps you to build a bridge to that customer or a perceived relationship with that customer. One method of giving information without scaring the prospect is to offer a free market evaluation over the phone. This is a very risky endeavor, however, because inevitably, the customer believes their home is worth more than it truly is. If you advertise or market that you will provide free over-the-phone evaluations, you need to be careful not to actually give a specific price on the phone: *"I'm sorry, I can't be more exact without actually*

Loren Keim's Compelling Buyers to Call

looking at the home, but I can certainly email you or drop off comparables in your home's size and age range for your review."

Some software packages, like Top Producer's Market Snapshot, which can be purchased for a monthly subscription, provide an entire report for a customer automatically including local market trends, prices, asking versus selling price, time on market and community information.

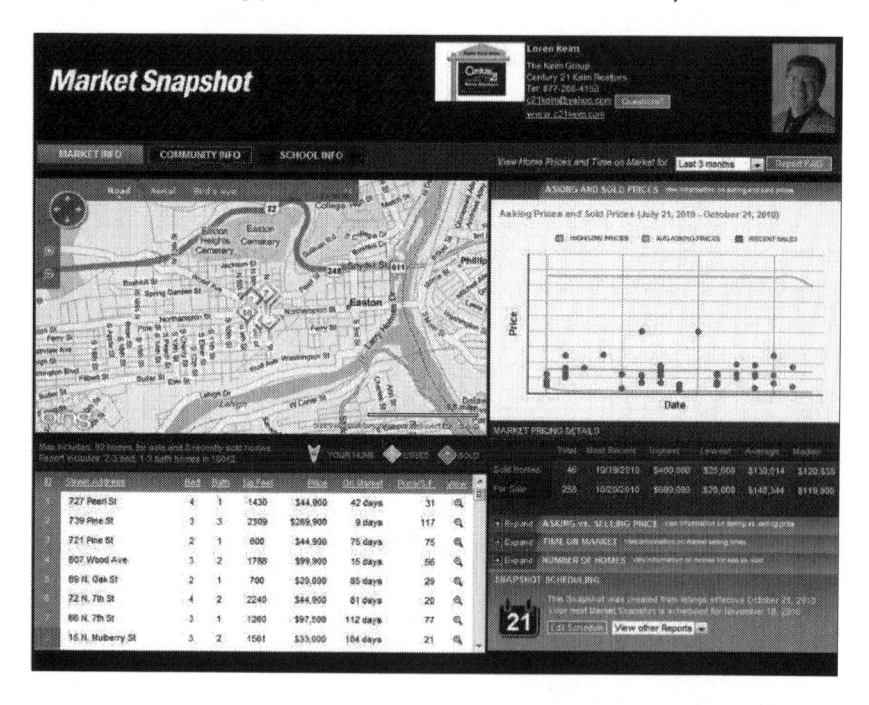

The Market Snapshot system stays in touch with the client, providing them with continual updates of listings, sales and trends in the market area defined by the customer. Marketing for this program can be included on your website, on social media platforms, in e-newsletter links and anywhere else.

Loren Keim's Compelling Buyers to Call

Automatic Listing Updates

Buyers want information on properties as they come on the market. Many buyers also don't want to be *"bothered"* by *"salespeople"* calling them. You can offer something of value by providing them with a steady flow of properties as they are listed for sale. Most real estate companies or multiple listings systems now have some form of an auto prospecting system which allows listings to be automatically sent to the clients based on the criteria entered in the system.

There's also a secret you should know about marketing your auto prospecting system: even though virtually every Realtor in the United States can offer this service to their clients, most home buyers don't know about it. Realtors mistakenly assume their clients know about their tools. They don't.

Because few agents are promoting their automatic listing update systems, you can market it as an exclusive tool.

> **New Home Seeker Computer System allows buyers to find out about homes the DAY they go on the market for sale!**

A more powerful approach may be to show potential buyers that they may lose the best deals if they don't become part of some search system. Fear of loss is a far more powerful motivator than the desire for gain.

Hundreds of clients call our offices each year asking to be put on the secret list of buyers for foreclosure properties. Foreclosure listings, of course, are generally put on the open market because banks realize that the open market generates a higher price than simply trying to sell a

Loren Keim's Compelling Buyers to Call

home to a few investors at a steep discount. Despite the reality that banks use Realtors, buyers everywhere seem to think that these *"great deals"* are being hidden.

Try to apply the same emotional technique to your automatic listing updates. What buyers want are great deals. The truth about great deals is that they seldom last on the market long enough to be advertised in homes magazines where they will be seen by many buyers. Even in slow markets, there are still *"hot"* listings.

Secret System allows some home buyers to beat everyone else to the best hot new listings!

Did you know that the very best listings never make it into Homes Magazines or the newspaper? They're scooped up by buyers with an inside track, by investors or by Realtors. Foreclosed properties, estates, and all the hottest deals in the local real estate market go fast.

Now, you may have an opportunity to become part of this exclusive club of buyers, by using a new super computer program used by Beauty and the Beast Real Estate. The Home Seeker System allows...

You can increase your response to this program further by lowering the barrier of resistance to the prospect. As you write your article about this incredible computer system, include that the customer will not be bothered by calls from a real estate agent. The buyer can simply call you when they see a property that they may have interest in.

Even if you promise not to call, you are collecting the names and information on buyers who want to purchase. Your goal is to find a way to follow up. Be honest in your responses. When a customer emails and tells you they want to be added to the program, make a follow-up phone

Loren Keim's Compelling Buyers to Call

call to them in order to thank them for joining the system and ask questions to get a clearer picture of their needs. This accomplishes the additional task of beginning to build rapport with the client.

> Agent: *"Mrs. Hall?"*
>
> Client: *"Yes?"*
>
> Agent: *"Hi, this is Peter Parker from the Web Agency. You filled out our online form to become part of our exclusive home seeker program. I won't take up much of your time. I wanted to thank you for filling out the form, and I just wanted to ask you a few questions to get a better picture of what you're looking for. The more information we have, the better we can program our computer to search for you. Would it be okay to ask you a few questions?"*

Summary

Our ultimate goal in any marketing is to entice a potential client to raise their hand to let us know they're thinking of buying or selling. One method that works effectively to attract these potential clients is by offering the customer something of value, or a fair trade that lowers the barrier of resistance a client has for calling you.

Something of value may be a free report or guide that will help their specific situation. Making an offer of a free report or free information with a compelling headline is a broad means of appealing to a larger audience than the typical individual property ad or image ad.

Chapter 5 - Target Markets and Unique Selling Propositions

I've just spent an entire chapter telling you to broaden your marketing to attract the maximum number of buyers, but targeted messages can also be effective depending on how they are used.

Remember that our goal in this program is to help you generate the most buyers possible. While a broad message like "*The 17 Deadly Mistakes Home Buyers make when buying their first home*" will appeal to the broadest possible audience, a message like "*The 7 Simple Mistakes Made by Horse Farm Buyers That Cost Them Thousands of Dollars*" will set you apart as the specialist in that particular market. If you are the specialist, potential clients are more likely to identify with you.

Selecting Your Target Market

When I opened my first real estate office in Allentown, Pennsylvania, I was competing with a huge company that advertised their

Loren Keim's Compelling Buyers to Call

firm was involved in one out of every four sales in my marketplace. There were many real estate companies and offices, but one stood out as the giant that we all had to compete against. This huge independent real estate firm, which we'll refer to as "M", had hundreds of agents, their own real estate television show and marketing brochures that I could only dream about.

So why bother competing? Partly because I didn't like the corporate feel of the large company, but mostly because I wanted complete control over my own transactions. I'm sure my ego figured in there a bit as well.

Since I was too small to compete head to head with such a behemoth, I dusted off my copy of the book *"Marketing Warfare"* by Reis and Trout, a book I highly recommend, and went to work on guerilla tactics for building market share. Reis and Trout explain that a small company should find niche markets. Clients like specialists, or someone who understands their particular market. A particular market can be a type of property, a particular area, or a combination of both.

We searched to find areas of real estate specialization that appeared to be ignored by the larger companies. The first target we selected was *Historic Homes*. Pennsylvania has plenty of stone Farmhouses, post-revolutionary brick Colonials, Victorian homes and many other unique dwellings with character. In order to attack this market, we began compiling a list of all the historic properties in the Lehigh Valley market area, where Allentown is located. At the time, we had to do this research from microfiche records because computer and Internet databases didn't yet exist.

In order to target this market, we started mailing letters asking them to call us if they were shopping for a "Historic Homes Specialist". The calls were few and far between. We decided to improve our message by giving the group something of value. We created a specific newsletter

Loren Keim's Compelling Buyers to Call

that we mailed to the group that had information on other historic homes, information on restoration techniques and other articles that owners of this type of property may find useful. We found that these newsletters had a much longer "shelf life" because the owners would hold onto them, and it dramatically increased our response.

Next we started setting up free workshops that would be of value to our target group of historic home buyers and sellers. I remembered attending a speech by the market guru, Jay Abraham, who explained that a salesperson can be perceived as an expert in a particular market or in a specific product by giving lectures or workshops.

We researched restoration projects and designed our free workshops to provide information on restoring historic homes. We provided tips to keep period character with modern functionality, and we even held seminars on financing these homes.

Finally, we sent announcements to the press explaining that we were the historic home specialists. The largest local newspaper, *The Morning Call*, ran a full page article about our team on the front page of the Real Estate section. Other magazines, such as *PowerSource*, also quoted us as the experts on historic property.

Although my team and I had learned a significant amount about historic homes, we had known very little when we first selected that audience as a target market. We had to research the marketplace and the needs and concerns of buyers, sellers and property owners in order to fully understand how to help them.

Our second target was equestrian properties. Like historic homes, we felt this group was not being specifically targeted. We researched the wants and needs of horse owners and created a marketing program that included advertising in equestrian magazines and a newsletter that went out to prospective horse farm buyers. As the

Loren Keim's Compelling Buyers to Call

World Wide Web came online, we created several websites that specifically targeted horse farm buyers and sellers. You'll find many of my articles on buying and selling farms all over the web today.

This program of targeting specific groups and creating a marketing program specifically designed to their needs was repeated with restaurants, liquor licenses, bank foreclosure departments, luxury properties, investment properties, corporate relocation departments and many other target groups. By the time we had completed our fifth or sixth target market, we had market share in virtually every part of our market area.

Remember that you *are* your own real estate company. Your firm may have the largest or smallest market share in your local market, but your personal market share will determine your personal income.

Specialization is one way to overcome the competition. When you're sick, you look for a specialist and when you're planning to buy a property, you want someone who understands your particular type of property or neighborhood and has a track record of success. You want someone who really knows what goes on in the neighborhood and what properties will hold their value if there's another downturn.

You may want to select your target markets based on your past experience. If you have past experience restoring homes, you may want to target the historic homes market and create free reports for historic home buyers. If you're an avid golfer, you may want to target golf course communities and figure out how to appeal to that buyer.

Certainly, you should select your target market or markets based on where you believe you can make money, but you should be sure to select groups that *you* would want to work with. Find out what that group or market wants and needs and how you can deliver it to them.

Loren Keim's Compelling Buyers to Call

A Sampling of Buyer Prospecting Markets

- **For Sale by Owners as Buyers** – Owners who want to save the commission or don't trust a Realtor to handle all the details properly. Those few Realtors who prospect this group often do it to show the owner why the agent can do a better job. What if you simply approach them from the perspective that most of them are going to be buying after they sell. Can you help them find that new perfect home?

- **Just Sold Buyers** – If you sell a first time home to someone leaving an apartment complex, they become the perfect catalyst for generating more buyers from that complex. Create a postcard that shows the home their former neighbor purchased and how much it cost per month. On the back, tell a short story of the purchase and how they can get a free report that can help tenants to stop throwing away money in rent.

- **Life Events** – Announcements in the newspaper let you know when someone is planning a wedding, had a new baby or passed away. Each of these life changing events leads to a change in housing needs. These groups may be carefully contacted to determine their motivation and needs.

- **Apartments / Renters / First Time Buyers** – Although there are lifelong tenants in every part of the country, the average renter in many places rents for less than 3 years. Direct contact with this group can net many prospective buyers who will be looking for a home very soon, even if you haven't sold a home to someone in the complex.

Loren Keim's Compelling Buyers to Call

- **Sphere of Influence** – This is a key critical component to your success. Building your personal database of friends, relatives, associates and past clients is very often the largest part of any successful Realtor's income stream. Each person you know has many other friends and relatives who they may refer to you. I highly recommend this group as your first target market.

- **Investment Property Owners** – There are several types of investment property owners. One type is continually looking to add to their portfolio of properties. These investors may become a great source of consistent income as they buy more properties. The second type is made up of owners of investment property that find it to be more of a hassle than they originally bargained for to own and manage real estate. These can be lucrative sources of listings as well.

- **Demographic Groups** – Similar to geographic farming, a demographic group is a group of people in the same industry or with the same likes. You may specialize in working with doctors or attorneys. You may specialize in clients who are Veterans of a war or any other group. Some popular demographic groups include newlyweds, seniors planning retirement or empty nesters, and young families.

- **Third Party Relocation Companies** – Millions of employees are relocated around the globe each year. Some companies, like Cartus and Prudential, buy homes from employees being relocated by large companies. Other relocations companies, like International Relo, simply help manage the move. The fees to work in this arena can be very high, but the leads tend to be very good. If you're interested in corporate relocation, consider joining the ERC (Employee Relocation Council) and begin learning all you can about corporate relocation.

Loren Keim's Compelling Buyers to Call

- **Personnel Departments** – The personnel director or human resources director knows who is being relocated into or out of the area. For small or medium sized companies with several offices, you may be able to offer relocation assistance.

Target Markets by Specific Type of Property

- **Equestrian / Horse Property** - Animal friendly properties are a large target market in many parts of the country. Customers are looking for a place to call home for themselves and their horses, alpacas, or some other large animals.

- **Historic Homes** – Farmhouses, Victorian Homes, Tudor Homes, Log Homes, Homes with Character are all part of the historic home property type. Buyers of this type of property often purchase the property due to their love of the history, the character or thoughts of a simpler time.

- **Green Homes / Healthy Homes / Natural Homes** – One of the fastest growing market segments. Consumers are more conscious of their health and want to make sure their homes are health-friendly. Specialty builders across the country are beginning to look at this growing target market.

- **Contemporary Homes** – While some buyers look for homes with the character of an earlier era, other buyers are actively looking for the unique, the dramatic and the contemporary in their living accommodations.

Loren Keim's Compelling Buyers to Call

- **Senior Communities** – Although this can also be considered a demographic group, senior communities of single story town homes, singles and condos are becoming more and more popular across the United States and around the world. Understanding the market for these can help you to build a strong long term business because seniors know other seniors who are also considering this lifestyle.

- **Special Location Homes** – Some agents specialize in golf course homes (homes on golf courses). Other agents study and understand the nuances of waterfront property. Special locations can include mountain top homes, view lots, beach front, lake front, park front or nearly any other premium location.

Using a USP – Unique Selling Proposition

A Unique Selling Proposition, as applied to a real estate agent or broker, is a position you create in the eyes of the consumer that you are unique among your peers. In other words, a consumer may come to you first because of something specific you offer. This is taking the target market concept to a higher level.

Have you ever been frustrated by a discount real estate firm that advertises they offer the same services at a reduced fee? That is simply a real estate firm creating a unique selling proposition and positioning themselves differently in the minds of the customers who contact them. The truth, we know, is that some of these firms advertise teaser commission rates, and up-sell the customer when they include access to the multiple listing system, advertising and paying a buyer's agent.

A successful full-service agent can often explain the difference between a discount broker's program and their own full-service program and list the property. However, in many cases, the full-service broker

Loren Keim's Compelling Buyers to Call

doesn't even get to play in the arena. The prospective home seller may *only* call the discount broker because their perception is that the discount broker is offering the same service at a discounted rate. This is a Unique Selling Proposition.

The same can be said of real estate agents who successfully secure a niche market, such as horse farms, historic homes or green homes. A client may call *only* the agent in the niche market because their perception is that the niche agent has more knowledge and can therefore get the property sold more quickly and for more money, or help them find the perfect property that meets their needs because the agent really knows that market.

For a USP to be effective, it should be short and memorable. A USP won't work if it's a paragraph long. It should be something that can be added to your business card, your personal brochure and any other literature you send out. Your USP should be boldly listed on your website, and in marketing that you direct at the target group your USP relates to.

Unique Selling Propositions for real estate fall into four broad categories:

1 – Niche Market USP

The goal with a "Niche Market USP" is to create the image that you are *the* specialist or expert in one area of the market. For example, you could be *"The Equestrian Property Specialist"* if your niche is horse property. You can offer free information on buying horse farms and may offer a free service to "search for the perfect equestrian property." Each will attract buyers.

Loren Keim's Compelling Buyers to Call

For seniors, you might get the Senior Relocation designation. You might advertise that you help seniors with their specialized needs in acquiring the property that is perfect for them in the community that suites them best.

Everything you do to that market should have a tag line that identifies you as the expert. Perhaps you'll be the waterfront property specialist, or a green homes consultant or a haunted home expert.

Incidentally, you'll need to check with your local state Real Estate Board or Commission to determine what you may or may not state in advertising. For example, in California and New Jersey, there are rules against calling yourself an expert without having some sort of certification.

2 – Unique Service USP

Many agents get confused when I talk about Unique Service offers because they believe that every agent can do exactly the same things. That's true, for the most part. However, most agents don't craft marketing around the emotional hot buttons of their customers. A perfect example is the automatic listing program. *"Find out about every property the day they're listed before most buyers know they're for sale with our free home search computer system."* You are making an offer of something that is not typical of other marketing and advertising.

"Find out about foreclosed property first with Steve Furst" is a Unique Service USP. If you're the go-to person for finding loans with no money down, your USP might be *"The No Money Down Specialist"*, or *"Call to find out how to buy a home with little or no money down!"* If you plan to only work with buyers, you may use that as a tag line "*I work 100% with Buyers*" or "*I work on your behalf, not the sellers!*"

Loren Keim's Compelling Buyers to Call

Another unique service approach is when you're working as part of a team. Your unique service becomes *"Hiring me is hiring a full team of expert professionals. Don't get stuck with 'just an agent'!"*

3 – Service or Performance Guarantee

A guarantee of your service is a unique competitive advantage that will separate you from the average real estate agent. ERA has used performance guarantees very effectively in advertising. *"If your home doesn't sell, ERA will buy it!"* Customers, who may not have heard the ad for several years, still remember it.

Examples of performance guarantees include:

- If you're unhappy with my service, you can cancel the listing (or buyer agency contract) at any time!

- I guarantee to sell your home in 90 days or I will charge you no listing side commission!

- If I can't sell your home in 99 days, I'll buy it!

- If I fail to call you with an update every single week, I'll give you $1000 at closing!

4 – Comparison USP

"Full Service for a Reduced Commission" is a comparison USP from a discount brokerage. You can compare yourself with your competition in many ways, although these are often used for sellers, such as:

Loren Keim's Compelling Buyers to Call

- My listings sell for an average of 99.2% of list price!

- On average, Ted's listings sell for 2.2% MORE than other homes in the market!

- Our team's listings sell an average of 30% faster than the competition's listings!

Using the concept for buyers might include:

- My buyers pay, on average, 7% less than list price.

- I negotiate on *your* behalf, successfully getting you the lowest price and best terms of any Realtor in my market.

Summary

Simple marketing messages offering service, or depicting you as a top agent in the area, are unlikely to produce many results. Every opportunity to contact potential clients is a chance to have that potential client read your message. Create a message from the perspective of what the client really wants, and give the message an emotionally powerful headline that will cause the prospect to actually read the entire body of the message.

When marketing or prospecting to find potential buyers or investors, you are more likely to entice individuals to identify themselves if you offer them something of value. That something of value can be free information that is valuable to the client, such as information on avoiding mistakes in their sale or purchase, or information on special financing techniques, which we'll be discussing a few chapters from now.

Loren Keim's Compelling Buyers to Call

Other forms of value include free evaluations of their property or free information for buyers, such as a steady flow of listings through an automatic listing program. To truly improve your results, add a unique sales message or Unique Selling Proposition that will differentiate you from your competition.

Chapter 6 - Delivering Your Message

If we're marketing specific homes in a newspaper, magazine or online, the message we're delivering is that particular home. Taking our career to a new level, we expand our messages to include compelling offers of free information with a powerful headline.

You've now decided, correctly, that my message may have some merit. Perhaps you *should* create a few newsworthy headlines advertising free information or free reports. Maybe you should also select a unique selling proposition and target a specific audience to generate buyers.

What is the best method of getting your message out to the public? How can you locate those buyers for your messages? Should you run ads in the local real estate magazine, the newspaper or send out postcards? What delivery system works best to entice buyers to contact us?

Loren Keim's Compelling Buyers to Call

The Delivery System for Your Message

Our delivery system can be almost anything. We've used postcards, email, web marketing, social media sites, newsletters, e-newsletters and more. You can utilize the same techniques with any delivery system, but the method of applying the technique might change slightly.

Mailing

Our return on blind mailers to people we don't already have a relationship with has been about one tenth of one percent. Mailing to one thousand people may generate only one single lead which may or may not turn into a client.

Mailers can be effective in three circumstances.

1. **Mailing to people who already know you** – your sphere of influence and past clients are 3-4 times more likely to read your

mail than clients who do not know you. This type of communication is used to remind them that you're out there and hoping for their referrals.

2. **Mailing to the same group of people over and over again** – Farming by mail takes a long time to generate any response, but over time you will find that people will begin to remember you. This is a costly and difficult method of business development.

3. **Mailing value-added pieces with Compelling Headlines that evoke an emotional response** – as I described earlier, when you are standing in a checkout line at a grocery store, your eyes are naturally drawn to the cover of a tabloid featuring a baby with 3 heads. A shocking headline can often cause someone to open or read your letter.

Letters VS Postcards

Letters allow you to send lots of information in the same envelope to a prospective client. Letters can be effective if they are hand addressed and physical stamps are stuck to them. If the letters are printed from a program with a bulk rate stamp on them, they are less likely to be opened because the receiver already knows it's an advertisement.

However, if you are mailing to hundreds or thousands of potential customers, it is very difficult to hand address the letters. Some agents overcome this problem by putting special teasers on the outside of the envelope. *"Learn the 9 Powerful Secrets of Buying a New Home for Lowest Possible Price Inside!"*

Postcards are more likely to be read because the receiver doesn't have to physically open them. Postcards don't allow a lot of room for

Loren Keim's Compelling Buyers to Call

information, but that might be beneficial because you'll have to narrow your focus down to the most important point. Determine what unique strength or strategy you're trying to convey to the reader and put it on the card.

Emotional Response

Whether you're sending a postcard or a letter, your goal is to get the recipient to read your message and hopefully take action. The action you desire is for that potential client to pick up the phone and call you with a need.

A strong headline is more than half the battle in getting your message read by the recipient. Keep thinking about those grocery store tabloid headlines that suck people into buying the paper even though they know, deep down, that a live dinosaur was *not* really found in the New York sewer system.

For example, I wrote earlier in the book about sending *"Just Sold"* postcards to apartment complexes where your buyers may have rented prior to buying. "Just Sold", however, is not only a dull and uninteresting headline, but is Realtor-lingo instead of plain English. Try having a little fun with your postcards. One of our agents sends out postcards that read "Do You Know What Your Neighbors did Last Night? You might be SHOCKED!"

Is this card more likely to be read than the typical *"Just Sold"* card? Let me guess. You realize this book is about attracting buyers and you *still* are curious what John and Sally Miller did last night, aren't you?

Loren Keim's Compelling Buyers to Call

Do You Know What Your Neighbor's, John and Sally Miller from Unit 101-B Did Last Night??

YOU Might Be SHOCKED!!

Your goal in writing anything to a potential client is to get them to read your message. A strong headline helps to accomplish that task. On the reverse side of the postcard, you can explain that their neighbors purchased a home for a great price and a payment that isn't much higher than they were paying in monthly rent. The neighbors were able to accomplish this goal because they met Happy Harry the Realtor after reading his free report on how tenants could stop paying rent and own their own home with little money down.

Another of our agents used a card with the headline "Your neighbors got EXACTLY what they deserved last night! And YOU could be next!" Each of these cards uses the name and address of the "neighbors" in order to give the card credibility and because the recipient may know them personally.

Loren Keim's Compelling Buyers to Call

Your Neighbor's, John and Sally Miller from Unit 101-B Got EXACTLY What They Deserved Last Night!

And YOU Could Be NEXT!!

Again, everyone wants to know what John and Sally got that they deserved, right? Almost all of the recipients will take the time to turn the card around and read the message. The reverse side states that the neighbors bought a home for about the same as they were paying in rent with little money out of pocket, when they thought it was impossible in this market. If the reader is interested in the same kind of mortgage, they can certainly call you for a free mortgage availability analysis to determine what kind of home they qualify for.

By the way, if you haven't had a sale recently that you can use to create a postcard like these, borrow a client. How many agents in your office never bother to send out any "Just Sold" cards? Ask if you can send out cards. The text may have to be rewritten to say "The neighbors were able to accomplish this goal because they met our team here at Hogwarts Home Team. Call Jillian Petrucci for this free report."

Loren Keim's Compelling Buyers to Call

Testimonials and Evidence of Success Mailings

The public doesn't really understand what Realtors do or how we do it. There are still consumers who believe that Century 21 and Re/Max pay us by the hour to show homes. One extremely effective method of attracting clients is to visually show them what we do with the use of stories.

Testimonial letters or postcards are simply stories written about you by one of your clients. This third party endorsement of your services can be very powerful. A strong headline might read *"My Realtor Saved My Marriage"*. The body of the article might show how the husband and wife were arguing because they couldn't find the right property that fit both their needs. They switched agents and hired you, and you found their dream home quickly, helping to restore the sanctity of their home.

Perhaps a more realistic one is *"My Realtor Helped Me to Buy a Home with No Money Down"*. If you're targeting renters, they may be enticed to read through the article. *"Fantastic New Government Loan Program Helps Buyers Purchase Homes With Little or No Down Payment"* is another strong headline. Use a true story with a good headline.

How I Helped Wanda and Greg Buy a Home Despite Past Credit Issues!

Wanda had medical problems and for more than a year, she was out of work. Greg simply couldn't pay the bills on his own and after six months of struggling, they had to give their car back to the bank and renegotiate their credit card payments. But now, Wanda and her husband were finally going to have a home of their own, and be able to stop throwing money away on rent each and every month. Wanda was thrilled with the new home she was able to buy with a loan program my team introduced her to this past month. She didn't realize that a home could be purchased with her credit situation.

Loren Keim's Compelling Buyers to Call

You might also vary the stories that you use to show the breadth of your business, which we describe as our evidence of success. For example, I had a client that I knew quite well that had bought and sold homes with me over the years. At a fundraiser, he announced to me that he had just purchased a multi-unit building with a storefront. I was surprised, and asked him why he didn't call me to assist him. "Well, you don't sell commercial properties, do you?" Of course I do, but he didn't understand that.

How I Helped Brandon with a Short Sale

Brandon was in trouble. He owed more on the home than it was worth in the current market and he had been transferred to a new location in Dallas, Texas. He had only weeks to move. Our team went to work renegotiating the payoff of his mortgage in order to get him out of the property.

Pickles, Beans and Rice. Just tell a story when you're writing one of these evidence of success situations.

If you're sending out cards to past clients, your sphere of influence or anyone regularly, include one on how you helped a buyer purchase with no money down, how you helped a buyer navigate the waters of short sales to successfully close a great deal or how you helped a buyer to purchase an investment property in order to save for their kid's education.

Each different story you print is likely to set off bells in the reader's mind of someone *they* know who is in the same situation. You're more likely to receive referrals if customers understand all the various aspects of your business. Tell them what you do with stories.

Loren Keim's Compelling Buyers to Call

How I Helped Bill Bob Buy a Bakery!

Billy Bob wanted to be a baker, but he couldn't leave his job at the candlestick maker shop without risk of losing his entire income. He had been working at the candle stick maker's factory - known as the wax works, for many many years and was incredibly unhappy. I found Bill Bob a wonderful small business loan for his new venture and then I wrote this article that simply goes on and on without any sense whatsoever. I'm sorry, but you'll just have to write your own stories!

Newsletters

As with any mailer, a newsletter will only be read by some recipients. The best newsletters are ones that the recipient can readily identify by looking through their mail. If you put your newsletter into an envelope, the envelope becomes one more layer for the receiver that he or she may choose to not even open.

In order to maximize the number of responses you get from a newsletter, make sure to include several strong emotional headlines on the front page, with much of the meat of the material inside. Be certain that each newsletter contains evidence of your success as a real estate professional in the form of stories.

Finally, give anyone who reads the newsletter a reason to call or contact you. Each article can end with the offer of a free booklet, free informational pamphlet or any other offer that entices the reader to take the next step.

Personalizing newsletters with information on your life and family may help as well, but this technique is most effective when you're mailing to people who already know you. Several of our agents include stories about their kids in their newsletters. This generally will only be read if the reader is already familiar with you, such as a past client or a member of your sphere of influence.

The Gooder Group (www.gooder.com), who we introduced earlier, is one of several firms that supply newsletters with articles that have built-in calls to action that entice the reader to contact the agent for more information.

E-Newsletters and Email

There are positives and negatives to sending anything by email. The cost to email is virtually nil unless you're using an email service. Even with an email service, the price is far lower to email than to physically mail newsletters.

Additionally, email gives us a much wider range of content than physical mail. Nearly any message you can mail can also be emailed, but you can attach or embed audio, video and links in your email messages. E-newsletters that provide effective articles can include direct links to free reports. Direct links dramatically increase the likelihood that the recipient will ask for the report.

The negative to emailing information is that so many of us are experiencing email overload, and just as many recipients won't open a physical letter, a similar number won't open any email that looks like an advertisement. In fact, some studies indicate that more than half of all emails are deleted without ever being opened.

As with any mailing piece, you must be certain to include a strong headline that will evoke an emotional response or at least a curiosity that will lead to the recipient opening and reading your message.

Loren Keim's Compelling Buyers to Call

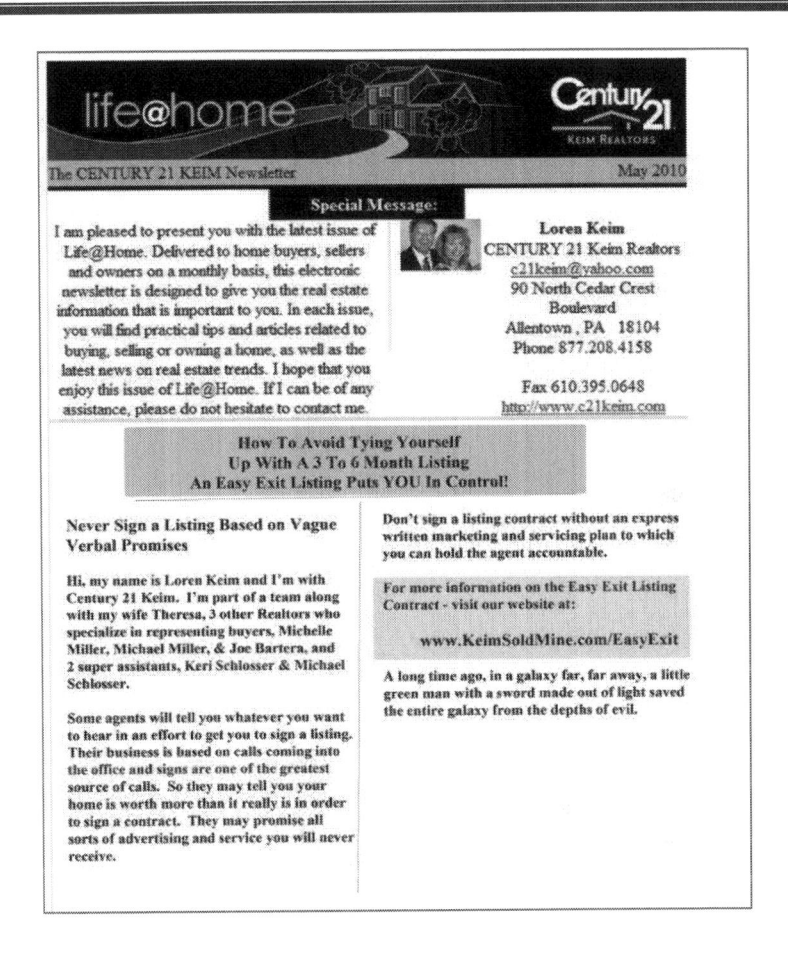

Email Tag Lines

Even when you're sending general emails to friends, relatives or clients, make sure to include compelling offers of free information in your signature line. Just below your name and contact information, create a postscript.

Loren Keim's Compelling Buyers to Call

PS - If you're planning on buying an investment property this year, don't do *anything* until you read our new free report "*The 11 Killer Mistakes Made by Investors and How to Avoid Them.*" This great report is available on my website at www.KeimSoldMine.com -click here for details!

Business Cards

Anything you give a prospective client should include a call to action, including the back of your business card. Some agents include a mortgage calculator on the back, because the client is hesitant to throw away the card. That's a great idea. Another might be to direct a client to your site for a free report.

> **Find Out the 10 Costliest Mistakes Made by Home Buyers and How to Avoid Them**
>
> **Free Report at**
> **www.KeimSoldMine.com**

Attracting with Promotional Products

"*Are you out of your mind, Loren?? I can't afford to advertise my listings this month. How can I afford to buy everyone a gift?*" The primary reason I mention promotional products as a form of marketing

Loren Keim's Compelling Buyers to Call

your services is that a potential buyer is far more likely to hold onto something of value than they are to hold onto a newsletter or postcard.

I also suggest that promotional products can be less expensive than many other forms of advertising. Promotional products can be used to remind customers that we're out in the marketplace, or they can be used as a direct response piece.

For example, we purchased flying discs (the generic form of the Frisbee) from Gideon Promotional Products for less than a dollar a piece, with our company named emblazoned across them, and gave them out at events. Kids and parents both loved them, which helped with our name recognition, but didn't necessarily produce direct results.

We re-ran the order, but this time including the headline: "Learn How to Buy a Home with Little or No Money Down." The ad still had our company name and included a website address for more information. We gave these away in apartment complexes and in heavy rental neighborhoods. Hits to this website dramatically increased, buyers called, and the give-a-way for 250 flying discs was less than the cost of a typical home's magazine advertisement.

Promotional items do not have to be expensive to be effective. Our most effective mailer includes a magnetic calendar with a tear-off page for each of the twelve months. These calendars retail for around thirty cents each, and stay on your prospect's and client's refrigerators for a whole year. Have you considered a calendar magnet to renters which has a headline about buying with a low down payment?

The sheer number of times a client has mentioned *"I see you every day on my refrigerator"* has convinced me that this is the single best item I send out each year. I urge you to consider, before any purchase, what will entice any recipient to take the next step and contact you or view your website.

Loren Keim's Compelling Buyers to Call

Agents in my firm send out everything from personalized pens, refrigerator magnets, key chains and jar openers to larger items like baseball caps, day planners and coffee mugs. Each item should be carefully considered to meet your budget and to deliver the proper message.

For example, a key chain may be thrown in a drawer and forgotten. A jar opener may also be placed in a drawer, but may be pulled out each time they need to open that pickle jar! Day planners, while expensive on a per planner basis, may be something the client will use every day for the entire year, and they could be looking at your name and message on the front.

Our agents have had fun with some of the items they've ordered. For example, an agent with our Allentown Marketing Center ordered fortune cookies with personalized messages. They very carefully wrote uplifting fortune cookie messages that dealt with the home, and then put their contact information and a direct response message on the reverse side, instead of 'lucky numbers.' When purchased in bulk, a box containing 4 personalized fortune cookies cost less than 60 cents.

Loren Keim's Compelling Buyers to Call

These boxes were a very inexpensive marketing project that was used as a follow up to *"For Sale by Owners"*, although they could have been used to farm apartment complexes or with your sphere of influence.

Popular Specialty items, imprinted with your name or your company name include:

- Seed packets for the Spring
- Personalized Pens / Pencils
- Rulers
- Measuring Tapes
- Buy a House coloring books
- Flying discs
- Baseball Hats
- Balloons
- Day Planners
- Desk Calendars
- Magnetic Cards
- Key tags
- Bottle Openers
- Wine Corks
- House shaped stress squeezies
- Emery boards
- House shaped letter openers
- Welcome mats
- And Many others

There are many online and catalog providers of specialty products. The one I've had the most luck with is Don Blose of Gideon Promotional Products. His firm takes the time to assist you in selecting the right product, and developing a message that resonates with your clients. Gideon's website is www.GideonPromotionalProducts.com and their phone number for a personal, no-cost consultation is 610-392-9149.

Loren Keim's Compelling Buyers to Call

Specialized or Targeted Web Sites

Targeting a specific niche market or offering a Unique Selling Proposition is a method to differentiate you from other agents. This concept can be applied to specialized websites that target specific niche markets. As I mentioned earlier in this book, my real estate team has crafted websites that target specific markets like horse farm buyers or buyers of historic homes.

Specific niche sites tend to rank higher on search engines because of the tight parameters of the information on the site and help to position you as the expert or specialist in that target market. On each site, you should post as much information on the niche topic as possible, including keywords specific to your market.

While you can add pages or sections to your primary website that target specific markets, as shown in the example below targeting buyers of foreclosed properties, you might also create a website specifically dedicated to the subject of buying foreclosures.

Loren Keim's Compelling Buyers to Call

You can create a simple website that is one page with an enticing headline, or you can create a more complex website with lots of information. Simple sites might focus on foreclosures, school information, first time buyer programs, luxury properties, historic homes, or nearly anything else you can dream up.

Loren Keim's Compelling Buyers to Call

Free School Information

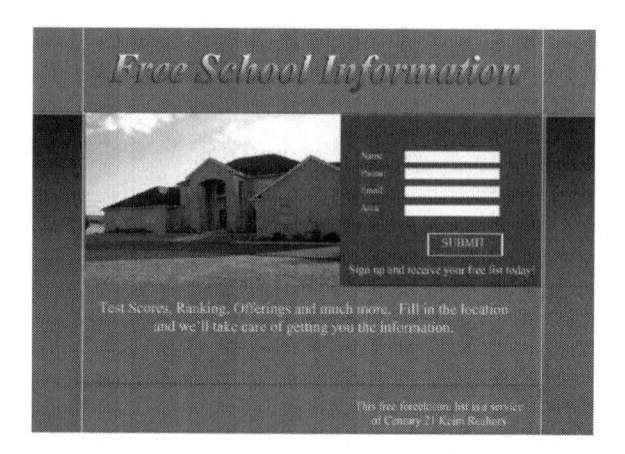

Test Scores, Ranking, Offerings and much more. Fill in the location and we'll take care of getting you the information.

This free foreclosure list is a service of Century 21 Keim Realtors

As I mentioned, however, niche sites that are packed with information and reports will attract motivated niche prospects and entice prospects to save the site as a favorite. Examples include the sites pictured on the next page, which you can purchase from the Gooder Group at www.RainmakerNicheSites.com[vii]. (No, I don't receive a referral fee. It's simply a great service).

Sites like Rainmaker Niche Sites are designed as informational websites that fly under the radar of many buyers because they don't look like typical advertising but still entice a potential client to identify themselves as considering purchasing a property. They give good information for a customer which leads that customer, ultimately, to visualize you as the specialist they want to work with.

The first site pictured is dedicated to buying foreclosures. It provides a free home search, entices the reader to sign up for a foreclosure hotlist, and includes free reports like "Picking a Real Bargain" and "Foreclosures to Avoid."

Loren Keim's Compelling Buyers to Call

Courtesy of Rainmaker Niche Sites

      Rainmaker Niche Site's First Time Homebuyer template, pictured on the next page, includes an entire section labeled "Real Estate 101" which is often saved as a favorite by buyers. Some of the many sections of this site include:

- Avoid Common Loan Problems
- 6 Tips To Buy More For Less
- Take Hassle Out Of Loan App
- Pick a Home by the Schools
- Down Payment Strategies
- How Your Credit is Scored
- Over-the-Net Home Finder

Loren Keim's Compelling Buyers to Call

- First Time Buyer FAQs
- And many more

The valuable information provided on sites like these create two effects. First, they help make the site 'sticky,' meaning buyers will save the site to their favorites as a reference, coming back over and over again. Second, the site positions you as the specialist, providing the visitor with valuable information, rather than simply trying to sell a home.

There are many pages on these sites that attract buyers to identify themselves to you by offering your services in finding the perfect

Loren Keim's Compelling Buyers to Call

home, being included in your hot list of properties, being preapproved for a loan and so on.

Chapter 7 - Social Media Platforms and Video

You can join social media sites and start posting information and building connections today without having your own website. There's a benefit, however, to setting up your website prior to really delving into the use of social media to build more contacts and create more business.

If you have pages on your website designed to tempt potential buyers and sellers to raise their hands and identify themselves, you can refer back to these pages in your posts on Facebook and other social media sites.

What *are* social media sites and why are they so powerful? You've probably heard of Facebook, MySpace, LinkedIn, and Twitter. You may have heard of Squidoo, Activerain and many others.

Social media sites are web based services that allow friends, neighbors, co-workers and everyone else to connect with each other. These sites allow people to join groups based on their likes and dislikes and share information. In many cases, they allow friends to share photos, videos, update each other on their lives and even play games against each other.

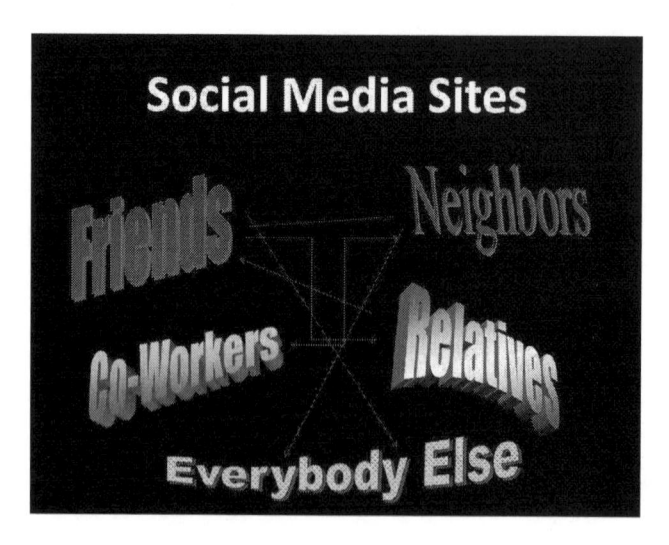

Social Media Sites
Friends, Neighbors, Co-Workers, Relatives, Everybody Else

Social media sites are very powerful for many reasons, one of which is the ability for customers to talk about you online. This can be positive or negative and it's probably happening whether you're there or not.

The emerging trend on the Internet is that consumers are slowly moving away from searching for businesses on Google and moving to asking their friends for recommendations on Facebook. There are *so* many false claims in the world that we no longer believe what we read. The person who ranks highest on Google may be the person who paid the most, and a majority of us realize that.

When we're looking for a service, we have all relied on friend's recommendations far more than any advertisement. If we want a plumber, rather than trust one out of the yellow pages, we ask a friend who they were happy with. We check out restaurants our friend's liked. We test the music they listen to and we ask for advice on finding the right Realtor.

Loren Keim's Compelling Buyers to Call

Because personal recommendations are much more powerful than advertising in the yellow pages, more consumers are turning away from Google ads and asking friends on Facebook for their recommendations of their experiences.

Facebook has allowed anyone to become a spokesperson to their friends. It's taking word-of-mouth marketing to a new level. They can broadcast an experience to all their friends, relatives and co-workers in seconds, and again, these comments can be very positive or very negative. This means you need to make sure your service is the best it can be.

Remember that Facebook is just a new tool to reach potential customers. You cannot abdicate your responsibility in working to find potential buyers and sellers in order to build your business.

Managing social media takes time. You have to dedicate time to it for it to be effective. It is also not simply a form of prospecting. If you simply go on to look for business, you will fail.

The Rules of Engagement

There are four golden rules for social media, which we'll refer to as the "Rules of Engagement."

Rule #1 - Do not use Social Media purely to sell! You will be ostracized and de-friended very quickly.

Rule #2 - Social Media is Networking. Networking is sharing with others, meeting others and building relationships that are valuable for all parties.

Rule #3 - Social media helps you to connect with people who can help you connect with others.

Loren Keim's Compelling Buyers to Call

Rule #4 - Remain positive on your social media activities because everyone can see them. If you complain about someone, lots of other people will see it or find out about it. Be the person you are, but also be the person you *should* be.

Facebook

Obviously Facebook[viii] is the hands-down leader, as of the writing of this book, in the arena of social media sites. That may change at any time, as MySpace[ix] was the clear victor only a few short years ago.

Creating an account is free and requires minimal basic information. There are several components to most major social media sites that, when utilized properly, can help you build your network and your referrals from that network.

Creating a Profile

Your profile is your personal information, including your family, your work history and your education, which helps the Facebook system, or any social media site, to find old friends who may want to connect with you.

Your profile should also have your likes and your interests, so you can find others who have the same interests or hobbies. Finally, Facebook allows you to include your web links. Be certain to link back to your personal site because Google and other search engines rank you partly by links, and this is a link from a major site.

Building a Network and Finding Friends

The key to building your personal real estate business long-term is not simply running ads and attracting new buyers for the rest of your

Loren Keim's Compelling Buyers to Call

life, but rather delivering exceptional service so those buyers refer you their friends, relatives and co-workers. This is growing your business through the power of networking and the service you deliver that network.

You can utilize social media sites to rapidly reconnect with everyone you're related to, you've met, or you've worked with through your entire life. You can also humanize yourself so this network sees you as a person rather than a salesperson.

One of the keys to developing these relationships is communication through the social media platform, but first you have to re-connect so that you have people with whom to communicate. On Facebook, you can pull down the "Account" menu, select "Edit Friends" and Facebook will open a window that assists you in making connections.

For example, the Facebook tools search your email contact list to see if any of them are on Facebook and then ask if you'd like to "Invite" them to be friends of yours on the site.

When you created a profile, you included your work history and your education. The system will look at your profile and point out that you may know some people from your high school or college that are close in age. You may also know current or former employees of any prior workplace. Facebook will build a list of possible friends, and you select which ones you'd like to try adding to your connections online.

To add any of the suggested connections as a friend, just click on "Add as Friend" and a request goes to that person to be linked back.

Loren Keim's Compelling Buyers to Call

News feeds and Your Wall

The first page you'll see when logging into Facebook and most other social media sites is a news feed. This is a list of posts by people who are connected with you on your social media site. These allow you to keep up on what others are doing and comment on what they are doing, which helps to solidify relationships.

In our screen shot above, you'll see two posts and comments on those posts. One is a post about playing Wii Bowling, with several friends or acquaintances clicking that they liked the post, and others commenting on it. The second post was about Hurricane Irene that had just blown through, and comments on that.

These posts are similar to group conversations. One person makes a statement and others comment on that statement or on others' comments. You can participate, which helps keep you at top of mind with

Loren Keim's Compelling Buyers to Call

your connections, by taking the time to comment on posts or at least clicking 'like' to let the poster, and those reading the post, know that you agreed or enjoyed the post.

In the upper right corner of the Facebook page are three pull-down menus. Home is where you'll find the news feed. Profile is both your personal page and where you can create your own posts. Account information, the third pull-down menu, allows you to change your settings and find friends.

The profile page, which is your personal page, includes a second set of choices including wall, info and photos. Typically, the initial page you'll see is called your wall. This is where you can post your own updates, thoughts and information about yourself. Friends can post messages to you here as well. It's a way to keep in touch and share information. These posts will show up on the news feeds of all your connections.

On the wall, you can write notes, but you can also add photos, video, announce upcoming events and even put in links. Again, we're not simply posting notes, video and announcements about our real estate businesses, but we do want to include them periodically to remind people, in a non-offensive manner, that we are in the real estate industry and we are the people to contact if our friends and relatives need help purchasing or selling a property.

Why should you add personal photos that others can see? You add photos because you want to connect with other people on a social or emotional level. You want to be their friend, and the person they go to when they need advice on real estate. You can do this by humanizing yourself. Post photos of your life, so they can see you in a different way.

You'll also discover that people like people who are like them. Dog lovers like dog lovers, and it gives them a connection outside the

Loren Keim's Compelling Buyers to Call

transaction. Mom's involved in school events share information. Golfers like others who golf and so on. So write something about your dog, your kids or your latest golf game and you'll discover that people will respond.

Social Media Sites

We Love Comic Books!
Musicians Rock!
We Hate Broccoli

I also like to periodically post humor or great quotes. The idea is to post something that will catch some attention and get response. You are building conversations and growing your influence *with* those conversations. Some of the lines I've quoted that have had the highest number of responses include:

> *Yesterday, I told my wife that a husband is like a fine wine; he gets better with age. Today, she locked me in the cellar.*

> Jack Handey: *"When I die, I want to go peacefully like my Grandfather did, in his sleep; not screaming, like the passengers in his car."*

> Maryon Pearson: *"Behind every successful man is a surprised woman."*

Loren Keim's Compelling Buyers to Call

Wayne Gretzky: *"You miss 100% of the shots you don't take."*

Again, you'll also need to post non-threatening real estate information periodically. There are many ways to do that without actually using a sales pitch.

"Hi friends. Long day! I spent over five hours showing homes to a relocating buyer. Some of the homes were really poorly staged. It is SO important to make your first impression your best possible impression. I had to bite my tongue a few times, because I would really have liked to give the owners some advice on how to make the home show better, but that would be stepping over the line, since I am not representing them. I'm surprised more Realtors don't take the time to educate their clients on staging."

This is showing your connections what you do in a conversational way. Once you've developed your message, press "share" and add it to everyone's news feed.

Periodically you might post listings for sale. As long as it's done in addition to other posts, your friends and acquaintances are less likely to see you as trying to sell them something. Postlets, VisualTour, Top Producer, and other software I've introduced in this book, have 'share' buttons that allow you to easily post your listings or information on Facebook, with links back to watch the visual tour or view the entire listing.

If you can't think of anything to post, you can always try finding real estate information outside of Facebook and reposting it onto your page. For example, the National Association of Realtors owns a site called "*HouseLogic*" which includes free tools and information. The site features many great articles about Financing, Home Improvement and everything real estate related.

Loren Keim's Compelling Buyers to Call

Look for a good article to repost on your Facebook or social media page that might be informative. This week I posted an article I found in *Houselogic* about reverse mortgages. Under the "finance" tab, where I found the article, there is a little 'F' for Facebook.

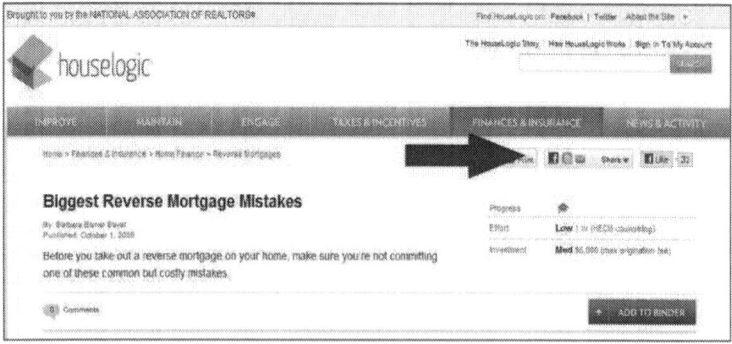

© Copyright 2011 NATIONAL ASSOCIATION OF REALTORS

Click on "share" next to that F, and the computer opens a new window to allow you to easily share the information on your page. The program will even carry over a photo from the article, a link to it, and allow space where you can write your own comments about the article on your Facebook page.

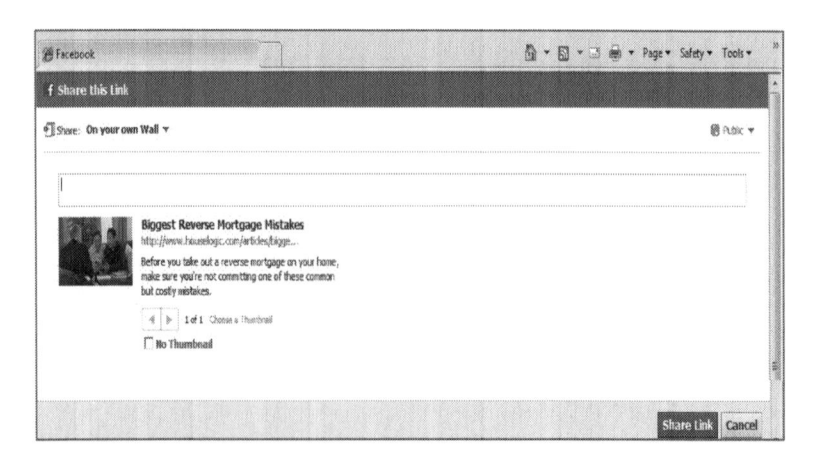

Loren Keim's Compelling Buyers to Call

Posting Events

You can either post events as a line on your wall on your profile page, or you can go to your home page and directly post an event and invite people to attend.

On your home page, in the upper right corner is a blank white space under the words 'upcoming events.' Clicking in the white space will open a window that allows you to add the title of the event, date, time, location and who should attend as well as details. Once an event is posted, you can invite people from your network.

This is great for posting open houses or broker's open houses if you have a lot of Realtors connected to you on your page. You might also use this for posting First Time Home Buyer events or Free Investor Workshops. Maybe you want to partner with a mortgage broker and do a workshop on whether it's better to downsize your home or take out a reverse mortgage.

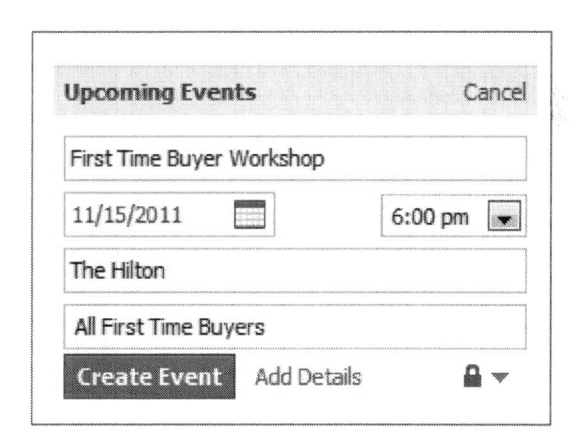

Loren Keim's Compelling Buyers to Call

Direct Response and Facebook

Your personal Facebook page or any social media page is another great resource for potential buyers where you may post direct response messages that will link back to your site. For example, you might post:

Hi Friends! We have a new free report available called - "The 11 Killer Mistakes Made by Investors and How to Avoid Them." This great report is available free on my website at www.KeimSoldMine.com!

(Or)

"I just read a great new report - The Secrets Every Buyer Needs to Know about Purchasing a Foreclosed Property. If you'd like a free copy, download it at www.KeimSoldMine.com."

These reports, when used periodically on your page, will attract the attention of your friends, family and acquaintances and help position you as the expert with all the answers.

Ads and Pages

Facebook also offers the ability to advertise for a fee or to create a free page for your personal business. On the left side of the main screen is a link with a little orange flag, called "Pages."

In Facebook, click on the "+Create" button near the top of the screen. Here you can create a 'community' page or an 'official page'. A community page might be dedicated to a neighborhood or town, and allow you to invite others to participate in your community page. An official page allows you to create a local business, like a real estate office or your personal business, a brand or product or an artist. You would

Loren Keim's Compelling Buyers to Call

likely create one under Local Business - Real Estate to create a page for your personal real estate practice.

Simply name the page and start using it. The photo below is an example page I created for Pennsylvania Horse Farms for Sale. Each business page has its own photos, info and wall for posting.

So what is the benefit of creating a 'page' for your business? It allows you more latitude to talk directly about your business and others can become 'fans' of your business. You can post about great investment property deals, interest rate changes and other information that might be of interest to your "fans."

Targeted Advertising on Facebook

Finally, let's talk about doing direct, targeted advertising on Facebook. If you click on "Ads and Pages" on your home page, you'll find

Loren Keim's Compelling Buyers to Call

the primary advertising dashboard. Facebook allows you to specifically target your advertising.

Although you'll have to pay for targeted advertising, you can post your direct response messages here and hopefully build a client base from the most successful social media site in the world.

Advertisements are short, to the point, and show up on the far right side of a user's screen when they're logged into Facebook. Each ad has a destination URL, or a web page on your personal website that the ad links back to. For example, if you're advertising a "Free List of Foreclosed Homes," your link will be set to go back to the foreclosed home page of your personal website, or if you have a niche website, it will be linked directly to that.

Remember that every advertisement we run should be designed to entice potential clients to raise their hands and identify themselves as thinking of buying or selling, so we use the same types of ads like "how to buy a home with zero down payment" or "free list of foreclosed homes."

Once you've selected your message and designed your ad, you can specifically lay out who you want to target. In what city or state are you selling real estate? Who are the demographics? Do you want it to show up on teenagers pages, or just adults between 25 and 64 years old? Do you want men, women or both? College graduates?

Do you want only customers who have certain keywords on their Facebook profiles, like "horse" or "equestrian" for example if you're targeting the horse farm buyer market? You can even target *just* specific

Loren Keim's Compelling Buyers to Call

groups, like graduates of Lehigh University or people who work at Air Products.

Finally, you have to pick how much you're willing to spend on any campaign. Perhaps you're just starting this campaign and you want to limit the cost to no more than five dollars per day. You can do that.

You can select whether you want to pay for *impressions* or *clicks*. Impressions are how many people's Facebook pages the ad shows up on. You can pay a certain amount for each one thousand times an ad of yours is displayed on someone's page. The one I recommend is pay per click. It doesn't matter how many times the ad is displayed, you only pay when someone clicks on your link.

Facebook will compute what 'per click' fee the system will be likely to promote, but you can bid any amount per click. The ad stops running each day once the number of clicks reach that daily budget, so if I bid one dollar per click with a maximum daily cost of five dollars, five thousand people may see the ad, but the ad will stop running for that day once five people have clicked on it.

Twitter

The second giant currently in the social media arena is Twitter. Twitter is a conversation in real time broadcast across the web with only 140 characters per message. This is called micro-blogging. Twitter allows you to post short messages, thoughts, and your actions in a format that easily works with your cell phone.

Where Facebook is concerned with connecting with people and reconnecting with old friends, Twitter is ultimately a broadcasting platform. You may also set up multiple Twitter accounts, perhaps one for friends and family and one for your real estate business.

Loren Keim's Compelling Buyers to Call

On the main page, you'll see a space to post your message under the heading "What's Happening?" A post is called a "Tweet".

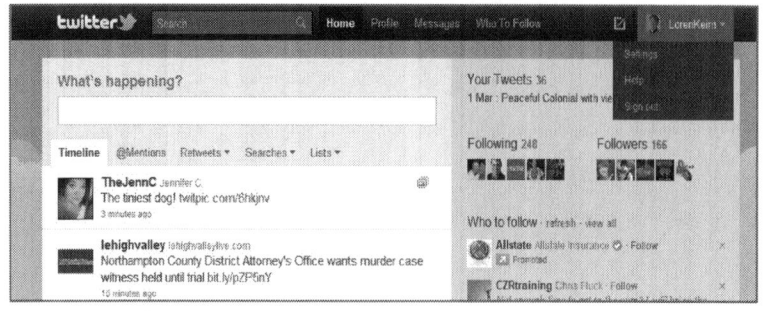

© 2011 Twitter

The main page of Twitter looks very similar to Facebook's News feed, containing the most recent posts of those individuals that you are following.

On the right side of the screen, you'll find those you are following and those who follow you. Unlike Facebook, no one has to confirm you as a friend. You can follow what's being broadcast by anyone. The Twitter etiquette dictates that if you are following someone, they should follow you as well, but it doesn't always happen.

Even on your profile, you are intentionally limited in what you can post. A very short bio that's easily read on a mobile device and only one link, so make it your best link.

On the main part of the screen is your most recent posts. I've done some sample posts on this account that each answer the question

Loren Keim's Compelling Buyers to Call

"What's happening". You can mention your free reports, or a new listing you have for sale.

The Twitter universe has its own language. @messages are direct messages to one individual - like an email or a text message, but through the platform of Twitter. The term "ReTweet" refers to reposting someone else's post that you find particularly interesting. Next to any post or tweet you view, you can find the retweet.

If you plan to post information on free reports and a link to the web address, remember that you're limited to 140 characters. There is a free service called TinyURL.com, which takes the long web address and creates a really short one for use with Twitter.

Finally, there's another service called TweetDeck, which displays all the information in a full screen fashion. The software is free to download, and lays out your Twitter account by friends, mentions of you, direct messages, and what's trending in the Twitter world, among many other features of this software.

LinkedIn

LinkedIn is another very popular Social Media site with its own relevance in the online world. This social media platform is designed specifically to work for professionals to exchange information, ideas and opportunities.

As with nearly any social media site, it is very easy to sign up and it's a free service. Like Twitter or Facebook, the main page displays recent activity of those connected with you. The main page of LinkedIn also allows you to create a new post. These posts can include your unique selling proposition or any of the direct response methods and posts we've outlined so far in this book.

Loren Keim's Compelling Buyers to Call

The difference between Facebook and LinkedIn is that LinkedIn is designed as a professional, business-oriented social networking site. The profile you create on Facebook will include likes, interests, hobbies, favorite books and movies and similar information. The profile you post on LinkedIn is closer to a resume.

Although Facebook allows you to include your professional experience including past careers, your LinkedIn profile summarizes your professional information from careers to education to affiliations.

One of the most powerful features of the LinkedIn platform is the ability to create groups. A group provides a good place to share information and ideas. On our Real Estate's Next Level page, we post information relevant to our organization and allow discussion.

Copyright 2011 LinkedIn

Loren Keim's Compelling Buyers to Call

I belong to groups for entrepreneurship, economic development, Lehigh University, real estate trainers, Century 21 groups and others.

In a section of LinkedIn titled "Answers," you can review what questions have been asked by fellow LinkedIn members and see if there's any question you might be able to answer, which helps you to build credibility. Looking over the categories of questions and answers you may find the answers to questions that were plaguing you as well.

ActiveRain and Broker Agent Social

There are also social media sites specific to Realtors. The two largest are ActiveRain and Broker Agent Social. While both sites are free to join, there is a charge for having your ActiveRain blog content posted to non-members and included on search engines.

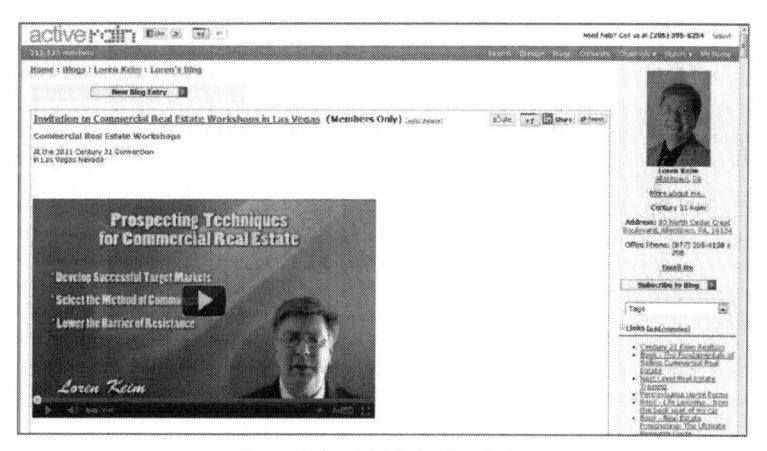

Copyright 2011 ActiveRain

The main page of ActiveRain displays the lead articles of the day that have been posted by other Realtors. This is the primary benefit of a

Loren Keim's Compelling Buyers to Call

social network specific to our industry. You'll discover a wealth of knowledge from other agents around the country and the world.

On the right side of the main page are links for business builders, followed by categories known as "Channels". There are consumer channels like home buying, home improvement and home selling, and there are channels for Realtors including mortgage finance, networking, online marketing and sales strategies.

Each state and local area has its own ActiveRain pages. If you subscribe to the site in order to allow the public to view your posts, you can use this service as a forum to post free informational articles that will attract attention and lead back to your site. For example, I might post specifically in the Pennsylvania section under news with my free reports.

ActiveRain also allows us to write our own blogs, which may include information on listings for sale, general blog posts and informative reports.

The other site for Realtors is BrokerAgentSocial. As of the writing of this book, BrokerAgentSocial is completely free and is a place where you'll discover articles by top trainers and blogs by Realtors around the country, including mine.

Other Social Media Sites

This book isn't directly about social media or online marketing, but social media platforms are great spots to test your marketing efforts. These services are also free, which allows you to drive traffic back to your website or to call you using compelling headlines and free information without paying a dime in marketing cost.

Loren Keim's Compelling Buyers to Call

There are many social media sites available to join, and we don't know which site may be on top a few years from now. The most popular social media platform a few years ago was MySpace, which is still a vibrant site for many users.

Other sites include FourSquare - a popular site due to its great applications for smartphones, GoogleBuzz which has integration with your inbox and is also smart phone friendly, Flickr which is primarily a site to host your photos, but can be used as a social interaction site as well. Flickr allows you to upload your photos and use them on other sites without paying for that service.

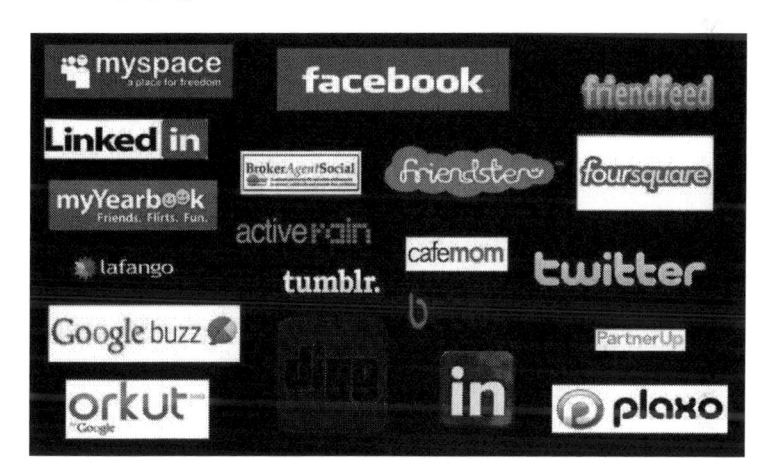

And of course YouTube, which is the world's biggest video hosting site. YouTube allows you to upload short videos of your properties for sale and link them back to your site, or create informational videos.

Viral Video Marketing

One of the objects of a career in real estate is to grow your business over time. A key method of growing your business is to build a steady stream of referrals by convincing your current clients, past clients

Loren Keim's Compelling Buyers to Call

and sphere of influence to send their friends, relatives and co-workers to you. There are methods to entice your current clients to passively refer you if it's in their best interest.

As I mentioned when writing about doing visual tours of a property, your client will send your information to their referral network of friends, family and co-workers as long as it is attached to information on their home that could lead to a buyer for that home.

Taking that a step further, YouTube is the second most used search engine on the Internet. If you can post a video of the property on YouTube, with a short message from you attached, and show your client the value of delivering that video to everyone in their social media network and email list, you can exponentially grow the number of prospective clients who view your unique message.

"Mr. and Mrs. Van Dersnoot, I put my listings on more than one thousand websites, on multiple listing systems and everywhere possible. I have no idea where the buyer will ultimately come from, but our goal is to get your home in front of as many potential buyers as possible. With that in mind, would you do me a favor? I'll be putting a video tour of your home on YouTube, the second most searched site on the Internet. Will you post a link to your home's video on your Facebook page and send out a link to the tour to everyone in your email list? Ask them if they'll repost it as well. The more people who know about your home, the more likely we are to sell it quickly and for the most money possible."

Applying that same logic to buyers, how can you entice your home buyers to send out your information to everyone *they* know? People are motivated by their own selfish desires. The selfish desire may be to sell their home, or in the case of a buyer, it may be to show off the home they purchased.

Loren Keim's Compelling Buyers to Call

Take the time to either create a virtual tour of the home your buyers are buying or create a short video and attach a message. Provide a copy to your buyers and gently suggest that they might show it to their family and friends. More often than not, they will send it to everyone they know. Even better, friends and relatives are curious about their new purchase and will play the video, which leads them to see your message as well.

Incidentally, creating video is not as difficult as you might think. Adobe Premier Elements is available for less than one hundred dollars and allows you to easily import photos and video into a single movie file, which can be uploaded to YouTube or other sites for free.

VisualTour, the virtual tour software I wrote about earlier in the book, also has a feature that will allow the tour to be uploaded as a video to YouTube and other video sharing sites.

The Next Level of Viral Video

You might also have a little fun with the video you create, which could lead to even more people viewing your message. For example, Mike Lefebvre, a Realtor in Franklin, Massachusetts created a two minute video of a listing that had tens of thousands of people watching. He designed the video as if it were a cheesy mystery. He is called to the home of his sellers who just experienced a supposed robbery of two steaks.

As Mike drives to the home, he looks out over the beautiful neighborhood and points out some positive features of the area. "With the K through 8 schools just steps away, the public wanted answers fast," he says. He interviews the owner about the missing steaks and goes to work searching through the home. Brilliantly crafted lines like

Loren Keim's Compelling Buyers to Call

"Somewhere in this 2200 square foot, 4 bedroom, 2 ½ bath hip roof colonial, there was a beef thief" allowed him to continue the story but point out the highlights of the home. "We dusted for prints on the newly finished southern pine floors in the custom kitchen" is another example of his technique.

Rather than a few dozen or few hundred people watching his message, Mike enticed tens of thousands to view with his unique approach. What video might you be able to craft that will garner that kind of attention?

Summary

First, we have to craft the message we're delivering to entice a buyer to contact us. Whether we're using compelling headlines promising free information or reports, or specific targeted messages to niche markets or enticing potential customers to call us with a unique selling proposition, we need to find the best medium or mediums to deliver our message

The system or medium to deliver that message can be virtually anything from postcards to email, web marketing, social media sites, newsletters or e-newsletters. The key, though, as Dan Gooder Richard would say, is to "make it rain." We need to create a plan to succeed in this business.

Christopher Reeve was quoted as saying "Either you decide to stay in the shallow end of the pool or you go out in the ocean." Stop waiting for that phone to ring and start creating your own destiny.

Chapter 8 - Utilizing Mortgage Products to Attract Buyers

What other methods might you employ to attract buyers to contact you about purchasing a home? How can you entice them to raise their hands and identify themselves as potential buyers? We've talked about compelling offers, free information, reports and target audiences for our messages. Still, there are some who will never call us because they don't realize they can buy or they are afraid to buy.

What is keeping some potential buyers from contacting us? Way back in Chapter One, I outlined that some potential buyers are afraid they will waste time and effort shopping for a home, only to be turned down for a mortgage, because many have heard horror stories about how difficult it is to get a loan approved. Other buyers aren't contacting us because they believe they need twenty percent down plus closing costs and they don't have that much in savings.

Loren Keim's Compelling Buyers to Call

Some who feel they probably *could* buy are afraid to take the plunge because they're afraid home prices will decline or that they will lose their job and don't want to be caught in either circumstance.

If we know the primary fears potential buyers have, and we know that the majority of those fears are unfounded, can we craft a prospecting and marketing plan, using compelling headlines and free information, that will entice them to learn the truth so they contact us to buy homes?

Mortgage products have often been a means by which we could differentiate ourselves from our competitors, if they are utilized correctly. We just have to understand the possible financing options and make those options fit with buyer's wishes. In the early 1980's, when interest rates were north of fifteen percent (15%), and that is not a typo, our team was able to sell homes effectively because we were able to negotiate better deals for buyers, which attracted more buyers through word-of-mouth referrals.

During that period, very few homes were selling because of the extremely high interest rates, and sellers were desperate to move. Many loans were held by private institutions rather than Fannie Mae, which meant we could actually go meet with the banks holding the mortgages. If, for example, a bank was holding a mortgage on 123 Privot Drive at 8% and the inflation rate was 10%, the bank was losing every month on that loan.

Writing a new loan would mean a 15% or 16% interest rate, which would put the lender into the positive column, but few buyers were willing or even able to buy under the circumstances. We *might*, however, convince the bank holding the note on that particular home that *if* the bank agreed to accept an 11% loan on that same home, higher than the inflation rate, they would no longer be losing money. If everyone else was advertising homes with 15% rates and we could advertise homes with 11% rates, which homes would buyers be more willing to purchase?

Even if the buyer liked one home better than another, the difference in payment would entice the buyer to purchase our listing. Obviously, we can't use this specific technique in the current environment, but you should understand that there are often ways around conventional thinking.

Throughout this book, I've tried to show you methods of thinking outside conventional wisdom. We are all limited or constrained by our beliefs and if we believe we can't find buyers, we are right. If we believe we *can* find buyers, we are also correct. We just have to figure out how to do it.

Low Down Payment Loans

A decade later, in the mid-1990's, when the market was again very soft in our area, my firm started a marketing program where we heavily advertised zero down payment loans or low down payment loans to renters. We used several very effective methods to entice people who never thought they *could* purchase a home to get pre-approved and ultimately purchase.

I'm not suggesting the creative financed loans or subprime loans that caused so many problems. In fact, I firmly believe that many of the crazy loans that were created by Fannie Mae were far too liberal in their lending policies and the practice led to our credit crisis. Our government had the brilliant idea that we could help those less fortunate by turning everyone into home owners simply by allowing everyone to buy homes with no money down, lousy credit and stated income (which translates into 'no job').

Loren Keim's Compelling Buyers to Call

Then when it all came apart, because social tinkering *never* works, the government blamed the greedy banks, who are only partly to blame for the financial meltdown. But I digress. You can read about that in my book, *Life Lessons from the Back Seat of My Car*, if you choose.

The loan I'm particularly referring to is the FHA program. Although the borrower needed 2.25% down payment at the time, the closing costs could be financed by having the owner pay them, which limited the amount of money a borrower needed to a required 3% of the total purchase price.

In fact, we were able to help buyers purchase homes with FHA programs for as little as 1% out of pocket because FHA allowed gifts from family members or non-profit organizations. Non-profits like Ameridream and Nehemiah appeared which allowed home owners to donate money to the program and the program gifted it back to the borrowers, which was actually legal. These programs have since gone away with changes in the FHA rules.

Unlike subprime mortgages, FHA still required solid proof of income, a solid work history, a decent credit score and an appraisal for the value of the home by an FHA certified appraiser. The difference was the down payment. Today, FHA requires a 3.5% down payment and Nehemiah-like gifts are no longer acceptable.

Having these low down payment programs available, however, is not enough. Buyers have to know about them and understand the benefits. We attracted buyers in several ways. We advertised in the rental section of newspapers. We put special signs on our listings, and we offered free reports on how to buy with little or no money down.

"That sounds great, Loren," you might say, *"but it doesn't matter because there are no low down payment loans anymore."*

Loren Keim's Compelling Buyers to Call

That is where you are wrong, and you need to think outside the box in order to help buyers to purchase homes. At the moment, FHA loans only require 3.5% down and an owner can contribute up to 6% of the purchase price toward closing costs, meaning a buyer can effectively purchase a $150,000 home with only $5250 out of pocket.

Compare this to someone who is considering renting a home. If they plan to rent a typical row home for $1000 per month, they'll generally need the first month's rent plus one month for security deposit. That means they need to have $2000. If they're buying that $90,000 row home under an FHA program, they'd need $3150, which is not significantly more, and the loan payment will be likely to cost them less per month than rent would on a similar home.

Imagine running ads in the rental section that spells out that you can own a 3 bedroom, 1.5 bath row-home on a quiet street for only $3150 down and a payment of $677 per month. Remember that you must follow Regulation Z and disclose how much interest is on the loan and other factors somewhere in the ad. Some potential clients will call because they think you're offering a lease purchase. Some will call because they're intrigued by the offer and didn't realize they could own for so little.

Are there 100% financed loans?

A more effective ad than owning a home for $3150 down payment is to advertise that you can own a home for zero down payment. Before you shake your head, thinking I've lost my mind, there *are* still zero down payment loans (at least in the United States). There are rural housing loan programs, veteran's loans and some community reinvestment loans or home owner's outreach programs.

Loren Keim's Compelling Buyers to Call

It is absolutely true that these types of loans are far more limited than the 100% financing programs that existed a few short years ago, but please keep in mind that we are attempting to identify potential buyers, not to sell every home with 100% financing.

Your job is to differentiate yourself from your competitors. Everyone knows about conventional financing and FHA. You need to spend some time meeting with local lenders and mortgage bankers to discover what loans *are* available that you may be able to utilize in your marketing to attract attention. You may learn of programs that will significantly benefit your pool of buyers and help you to generate more buyers and referrals from those buyers.

In the early part of 2001, my team was putting *Zero Down Payment* signs on many of our listings to attract attention. On at least two occasions a buyer contacted us to ask about the zero down loan and ultimately paid cash for the home. Why call on a 'no money down' ad if you have the cash? Even if the buyer *has* the resources to purchase, 100% financing is intriguing and creates buyer leads.

Rural Housing

Obviously, if you're a Realtor only servicing a very urban population, you may not be able to utilize any rural housing programs, but you may find some great community reinvestment loans. Rural housing loans or farm and home loans were created to help buyers in rural locations, but are often available for homes that are a close commute to population centers.

The Department of Agriculture's Rural Development mortgage guarantee program is not limited to farmland. Small towns, boroughs, and many suburban communities qualify for financing through the USDA

Loren Keim's Compelling Buyers to Call

program. In many parts of the country, USDA rural housing loans are available within a fifteen to twenty minute drive of an urban center.

The USDA has maps on its website that highlight eligible areas:

http://eligibility.sc.egov.usda.gov

Rural housing loans also have income limit restrictions, based on family size and location. You'll need to determine the terms of the loans that are currently available, the income restrictions on these loans, and the locations that qualify.

"But that home may not be in the exact location the buyer wants," you might say. Remember my story of selling homes at a lower interest rate than the competition in the early 1980's. Although another home may have appealed more to a buyer, they would select and purchase their second or third choice simply because the interest rate was so enticing. A rural housing program allows buyers the chance to own if they're willing to drive a little further, and they may discover that they like the rural lifestyle.

Secondly, our goal in marketing these loans is to identify buyers who are thinking of buying. They may not like the location that works with a rural housing program. They may decide not to buy with this type of loan program, but they are raising their hand to tell us they are considering purchasing. It's up to us to follow up with that potential buyer and keep with them until they purchase.

We may *never* have known they were thinking of buying without running a zero down payment advertisement because they may never have called us from one of our homes in the local magazine.

Loren Keim's Compelling Buyers to Call

VA Loans

VA guaranteed loans are specifically for qualified Veterans. These loans are made by private lending institutions, including mortgage companies and banks, and are guaranteed by VA.

VA loans do not have mortgage insurance, but *do* have a funding fee, although the borrower can roll the fee into the loan amount. The funding fee varies based on whether the loan is the veteran's first or a subsequent loan and whether the veteran served in the regular military or in the Reserves or National Guard.

The wars in the Middle East have helped to create many eligible buyers who may take advantage of this loan program. An advertisement might read "Veteran's - buy this home with Zero Down Payment!" or a sign rider might be placed on the home.

Again, although this "zero down payment" loan is limited to veterans, it is a starting point to attract buyers to contact you about purchasing with little or no money down.

Navy Federal

The Navy Federal Credit Union also offers a zero down payment program for qualified members. The eligibility is limited to members of the military, some civilian employees of the military and U.S. Department of Defense, and family members. Navy Federal is the nation's largest credit union in assets and membership.

Navy Federal's one hundred percent financing program is similar to the VA's, although Navy Federal's funding fee is currently less than the VA's funding fees.

Loren Keim's Compelling Buyers to Call

Community Reinvestment Loans

The future and fate of many community reinvestment loans is an unknown, but there are currently banks and lenders in virtually every part of the country that offer extremely low down payment loans to borrowers who qualify. These specialized loans are designed for low or moderate income borrowers or first time buyers.

Many of the loans have income restrictions, but they tend to be liberal enough that many buyers qualify. Some programs require the borrower to take a class on home ownership.

In my area of Pennsylvania, the Home Owners Outreach Program, is managed by a group of banks and lenders and allows a buyer to purchase a home with only $1600 in total funds. On a $120,000 purchase, that amounts to only 1.33% down.

Voice Mail Capture Systems

Attracting buyers with zero down payment loans has long been one of my toughest sells to agents. Realtors believe that advertising these loan products means they'll attract lots of unqualified buyers who will waste their time.

The truth is that you're slogging through unqualified buyers right now. What if we could create a system to exponentially increase the number of leads from buyers you receive? Even better, what if we find a way to help these buyers prequalify themselves so they don't waste your time? Finally, what if you could differentiate yourself from the competitors so clients would *want* to work with you and work by *your* schedule?

Loren Keim's Compelling Buyers to Call

Voice mail capture systems allow all that to happen when they're applied correctly to marketing. By a voice mail capture system, I'm referring to a commercially available service you can purchase for between fifteen and thirty dollars a month that gives you a toll-free phone number and a series of voice mailboxes where you can record specific messages about properties. For example, you may have a voice mail system with twenty mailboxes. When a buyer calls your toll-free hotline, they will be prompted to enter a mailbox number. Your advertisement will have a specific mailbox. The buyer will type in the extension and the message will begin playing for the buyer.

The benefits of a voice mail system:

- Attract more buyers - A voice mail system can attract more buyers to call, because the caller knows they're listening to a free recorded message and they don't have to talk to an agent.

- Self Pre-qualification - If the recorded message explains that a buyer needs to have a job and decent credit, the system eliminates your need to talk to the least prequalified customers that are calling you now.

- Pre-sells you as the expert – Your message, as we'll examine below, will explain that many real estate agents simply use the same conventional and FHA products over and over again and you have carefully researched all the available mortgage programs to discover the lowest down payment and lowest interest rate loans available because you're a caring and concerned Realtor who does your best for every client. This system will position you as an agent who cares and one who is more knowledgeable than others in the market, setting you apart.

Loren Keim's Compelling Buyers to Call

How are all these things accomplished? It starts with attracting a buyer by using a compelling headline about zero down payment loans or low down payment loans. This headline can be associated directly with a property, such as included in a home magazine ad or as a sign rider, or the headline can be done generically like in the postcards outlined in Chapter 6.

The next step is to create a gripping voice mail recording that the customer, having been enticed by the compelling headline, will listen to. The voice mail should have several components including information on the home, information on the loan program, a statement differentiating you from competing Realtors, a statement to prequalify the buyers and in closing, a call to action.

First, if you are tying the headline to a specific property, the message should state something about the home, but please keep that part of the message as generic as possible. I don't want the message to keep a good buyer from contacting you.

To digress slightly, remember that I outlined early in this book that most ads actually turn-off buyers rather than turn them on. The reason is that buyers look for reasons not to view a particular home. If the home has too few bedrooms, too few bathrooms, too small a yard, taxes that are too high or any number of other reasons, the buyer will not call you. Many agents insist on putting brochure boxes in front of homes with full copies of the listings. Again, this keeps many buyers from actually ever picking up a phone and calling you. This home may not be perfect for a particular buyer, but our goal is to attract all buyers to contact us. Then we can go to work finding them the right home.

With voice mail messages, we have to be careful to avoid that same trap. An opening might be: "Thanks for calling Loren Keim's consumer information hotline. The home you're calling about is a beautiful colonial in a quiet neighborhood in the Parkland school district

Loren Keim's Compelling Buyers to Call

with a nice size yard, a gourmet kitchen and located on a cul-de-sac. You'll fall in love with this home the first time you see it."

I realize that message tells the listener very little about the home. That's okay. Our goal is to identify buyers. The real key to utilizing a sign rider in front of the home or an ad in a magazine about a specific property to attract attention is to give them something else to consider.

The second part of the message focuses on the mortgage product you're advertising. "But what's even more exciting about this great home is the zero down payment loan program available for qualified buyers. This loan program, part of the USDA's rural housing program, may allow you to purchase the home with absolutely zero down payment." Obviously you're repeating yourself, but you want to be certain they are excited about the possibility of using this loan to purchase.

The third step is to differentiate your real estate practice from competing Realtors. "You may be asking yourself: if there are zero down payment loans available, why haven't I heard about them? The truth is that many Realtors don't even know about them. My team and I are concerned about providing the best loans to our clients. While many agents are likely to take you to a local lender who will provide typical conventional or FHA loans, we've spent countless hours searching through thousands of loan programs to find you the best rates, the best payment options and the best qualifying loans that exist in the market today. This has taken us a lot of time and effort, but it's part of our commitment to our buyers to get them the best possible mortgages."

The fourth step is to get buyers to eliminate themselves if they know they can't possibly qualify for the loan. "This program is exceptional and only applies to certain homes that qualify, like the one on Arrow Way. The program is also only available to buyers who have at least a moderately good credit score and have been employed with a stable income over the past two years."

Loren Keim's Compelling Buyers to Call

You'll notice that I did not spell out the income restrictions. This is partly because they change over time, but it is important to get the buyer to contact you so you can determine what program will work best for them. However, all those buyers who have poor credit and somehow believe they can buy with no money down will not take the next step to call you or be connected with the office. Likewise, those people are not currently employed will hang up as well.

Finally, you want the buyer to take action. Many of the commercially available voice mail hotlines allow the listener to press a button at the end of the message to be connected with your office or your cell phone or to leave a message for more information. "If you're interested in more information on this property or if you're interested in learning more about the low down payment or zero down payment options for purchasing a home, press the number 6 now to be connected with our team at Sign of the Bat Realty here in Gotham City."

Different voice mail systems have different features. Most systems have a call capture feature, which means they use caller-ID to create a list of the phone numbers of all callers to the service. This allows you to call back those who do not leave a message, if you so choose. Others include instant email and text notifications for the phone numbers for any incoming calls. There are even services that allow the caller to have a text message sent to their phone with the web address of a property brochure or virtual tour and others that will automatically fax brochures to the clients or automatically follow up to them with text messages.

I suggest choosing one that has toll free usage for incoming calls. Many of these hotline services charge on a per-minute basis for incoming calls. One of the services I've recommended is Hotline America, which can be found online at hotelineamerica.com. This service includes a free

Loren Keim's Compelling Buyers to Call

phone script library and is also offering a free month for readers of this book with the promo code "nextlevel" if you sign up now.

When should you use free recorded messages? I suggest only using them in conjunction with marketing of mortgage products or similar special incentives. Some Realtors use recorded messages on every listing in order to avoid having phone calls go directly to the agent. I strongly disagree with this tactic because I feel you have a much better chance of converting an incoming call into a buyer if you speak with them. The goal with this voice mail system is to position yourself as the expert and to attract buyers that may not have ordinarily called you, not to replace having a buyer speak with you.

I've been asked by Realtors on a number of occasions why they can't simply put the script on their website and direct clients to the web for the same information. Isn't that less expensive than having a hotline? Yes, it is cheaper, but the idea behind having a hotline is that you *can* capture phone numbers of those callers who listen to your messages. There are many forms of marketing that work well with this system including bright yellow signs, classified ads and online classified ads, laundry flyers and apartment mailers.

The Bright Yellow Sign Campaign

"*Geez, Loren, I was at a workshop ten years ago with Craig Proctor or Joe Stumpf or any number of other trainers, and was told about yellow signs.*" So was I. If you've never heard about using bright yellow signs, allow me to introduce them.

Our goal is to attract positive attention and entice a prospective buyer to take action, hopefully leading to the buyer identifying themselves to us. Putting a for-sale sign on a home will get the same reaction as every other for sale sign. Buyers will drive right past it, unless

Loren Keim's Compelling Buyers to Call

they are specifically looking for a home in that location, because there are so many homes for sale that signs are on every block. Real estate signs tend to fade into the background and may not be noticed, unless someone is actively looking. We want to attract the attention of those potential buyers who are not yet or not actively looking for a home.

We need to create a pattern interrupt in the consumer's brain to get them to swivel their head, read the for-sale sign and get them to take action. If signs only attract the attention of those buyers actively looking in an area, how do we get buyers to read our message? By making it stand out in an unexpected way.

After you set up your hotline, buy a half dozen 24" x 18" bright yellow signs. They cost about two dollars each. You're going to handwrite something on each of them that will catch a buyer's attention. Why handwrite instead of getting nice pre-printed signs? Because if you get nice pre-printed signs, they will look like real estate for sale signs or like political signs. You need to catch the attention of someone driving by. This is the same theory as putting balloons on open house signs. They catch attention. Handwritten signs catch attention. Our brains says "yard sale??" and we look to see what the sign says.

The message should then be every bit as compelling as a headline in any postcard mailed. I prefer using the headline "Zero Down Payment" or "No Down Payment" because both attract attention, but they're not enough. You've intrigued the reader. They're now thinking "zero down payment? How do they do that?" They still don't really want to take the time to speak with a salesperson.

The second part of the message then reads "Free Recorded Message" and gives your hotline phone number.

Loren Keim's Compelling Buyers to Call

> **FOR SALE**
> Zero Down Payment
> Free Recorded Message
> 1-800-555-1234 x11

The first time I tried this system it didn't work. I had heard about zero down payment signs and ordered fifteen beautifully and professionally printed signs for my hotline. I received three calls. When I started over and purchased bright yellow signs and hand wrote the messages, I attracted more than one thousand calls in sixty days from a dozen of these yellow signs. These signs are the visual equivalent of a compelling headline on a postcard.

The Classified Campaign

I'm not a big fan of using newspapers for marketing real estate in the current environment. (There goes the New York Times review of this book!) If you're going to run a classified campaign, this technique is far better than running any individual home. I would suggest running zero down payment ads in the rental section.

Newspaper classifieds still seem to bring calls from the rental section, and this may be a target audience that isn't currently thinking of buying a home, but may be convinced to buy with the right message. Ads should be carefully crafted to appeal to the largest number of potential future buyers.

Loren Keim's Compelling Buyers to Call

Lovely homes for sale in beautiful suburban neighborhood in Lehigh County. Zero down payment is required. For more information, listen to our free recorded message at...

Another approach is to use specific figures to directly compare other rentals on the page to your property for sale.

Available now - Own a 3 BR Townhome in East Penn S.D. for $1073 per month and only $1600 down for qualified applicants. For details...

Again, for this advertisement or any ad, you must be careful to follow Regulation Z. Talk to your favorite mortgage lender to structure an ad that meets the legal requirements.

Finally, you might give the reader a series of options. Find a home seller who is willing to either sell the home or rent it and run an ad like:

Rent or Purchase this lovely 3 BR Townhome in East Penn S.D. for $1250 per month. For details...

When we've run similar ads in the past, we received *only* callers wanting to rent a home, not purchase, of course. Our goal was to convert them to buyers, if possible, before the home was rented.

Client: "I'm calling about the townhome for rent in the paper."

Agent: "Okay, I'm pulling up that information now. My name is Dan Brown, what's yours?"

Client: "Web Griffin."

Agent: "Okay Web, I have that information. The owner is looking to either lease the property or sell it. Are you interested in renting or buying?"

Loren Keim's Compelling Buyers to Call

Client: "Renting."

Agent: "Okay. He's asking $1250 a month. We'd need $1250 for the first month's rent plus an additional $1250 for security deposit, or a total of $2500. Would that be an issue?"

Client: "No, I have that.

Agent: "Great. <pause> Just a quick question. The owner would really rather sell the home. Is there a reason you'd rather rent than buy?"

Client: "I haven't saved enough money down yet."

Agent: "Really? Actually, this home qualifies for something called a Home Owner's Outreach Loan. If you qualify, you could purchase it for about $1600 total cash out of pocket. That's less than the $2500 you'd have to come up with to rent, and the payment would likely be lower than $1250 a month, and you'd own the home. If we could find a way for you to own the home for less each month then rent and for less than $2000 out of pocket, would you consider purchasing?"

If we would run an ad for rent over a week period, we'd be likely to pick up more than one hundred rental calls on the home. If we asked each of them the same question, about ten percent of them would allow us to run a credit check and qualify them for a purchase. Of those ten or eleven potential buyers, two or three would absolutely qualify with no problem. Better, someone would almost always buy the home.

It happened, from time to time, that the home was rented rather than sold, but the majority of homes attracted buyers who didn't realize they could actually qualify to buy a home. Additionally, these buyers often became our best source of referrals because all their friends didn't think they could buy either.

Online Classified Campaign

There are dozens, if not hundreds of thousands, of online classified sites. Two of the most popular include Craigslist and Backpage. Small advertisements like those in the newspaper classified can attract just as much attention in the rental section of Craigslist and other classified sites.

Online, you may include some photos of a home, but keep the ad simple in order to attract the maximum number of potential buyers to contact you.

The Laundry Flyer Campaign

Where are the most effective locations to find those who are currently renting? If they are first time buyers, they may go to a Laundromat to wash clothes, where there is often a bulletin board. Move-up buyers, by comparison, may be at companies where a bulletin board may be found in a lunch room or near the water cooler. When you stop to think about it, there are many possible places to hang flyers.

Create a compelling headline. You might put a flyer together for a starter home and hang it at Laundromats all over town with a headline like "No Money Down and $877 per month to own!" with a sub-headline "Washer and Dryer Included!"

Loren Keim's Compelling Buyers to Call

You'll also want to make sure that no one pulls your flyer off the wall and runs home with it. You want to attract the maximum number of potential buyers, so the flyer needs to stay in place, but that the readers of the ad need an easy way to call you.

Try making up a flyer with pull off tabs at the bottom. Take a sheet of copier paper, print your name and number several times across the bottom, take a scissors and cut strips to create pull off tabs. Potential buyers can rip off the small piece of paper and carry it with them until they call you.

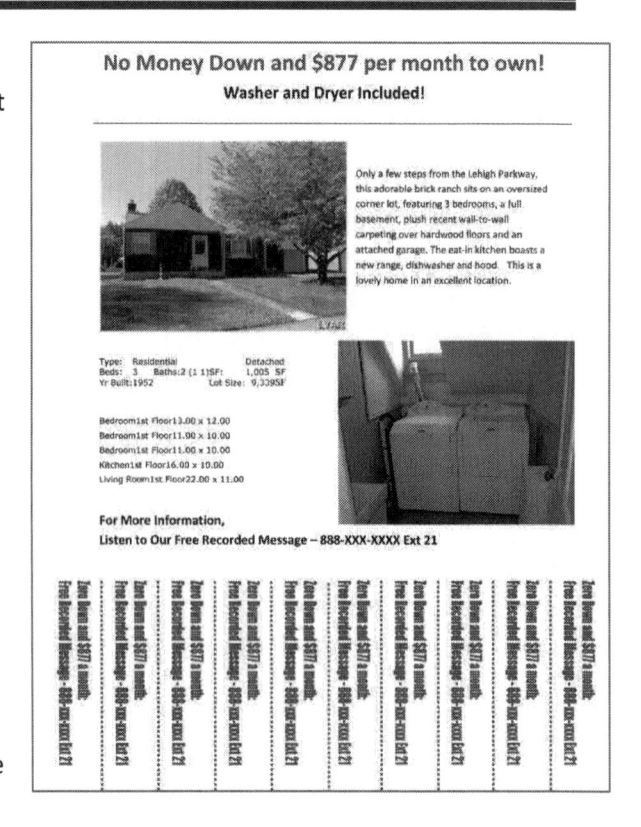

The Apartment Flyer Campaign

Obviously you can create the same format flyer for apartments, enticing the tenant with a zero down headline. Another might be to create a folded card that has an article on the front, like "New Government Program Helps Allentown Buyer Purchase Home with No

Loren Keim's Compelling Buyers to Call

Money Down" and as the tenant opens the card, you might have several homes with payments written across the top of the photo.

If a tenant can visualize owning a particular home for a payment around the same amount they're paying in rent, and realize they'd actually own that home, you're halfway to creating a buyer. Better, that buyer will ultimately thank you and refer others to you.

Will every home qualify for a zero down loan? No, of course not, but we're trying to find a way to attract more buyers. In order to use these marketing concepts, you may need to prospect for listings in areas that allow this type of loan, or perhaps you can borrow a listing from another Realtor for your campaign.

Keep in mind, however, that most homes will qualify for FHA financing, and those that are in poor condition may be used with an FHA 203k product to correct the defects.

**New Government Program Helps
Allentown Buyer Purchase Home with
No Money Down.**

Allentown, PA - Carmen looked back at her old apartment for the last time as she loaded her car with the last of her personal belongings. Carmen had spent 3 long years in the cramped apartment with her husband and daughter, Ashley. Recently, she discovered a new government loan program which allowed her to purchase a home with zero down payment.

Tears welled in Carmen's eyes as she considered the years that she spent trying to save enough money to buy a home of her own. At one point she thought it would never happen because the bills always seemed to be greater than her income.

Offers from Lenders

Some lenders have special offers that might attract attention and help entice a buyer to ask for more information. For example, one fear

Loren Keim's Compelling Buyers to Call

buyers have is that they'll lose their job just after settlement and be unable to pay the mortgage after shelling out thousands of dollars in down payment and closing costs.

Gateway Funding, a national lender, is currently offering a free insurance policy for buyers that will help allay that fear. If the buyer loses his or her job in the first year of the mortgage, the lender's insurance will pay up to one thousand dollars a month toward their mortgage for them, for a period of several months. There are some conditions and restrictions, but the offer certainly helps lower the barrier of resistance to purchase a home.

Gateway and several other lenders are also offering free home warranties with a mortgage, which reduces the concern of a buyer that they will be bankrupted by costly hidden defects in the home after settlement.

As a Realtor, you might partner with Gateway or another lender on marketing programs such as "Buy this listing and finance through Gateway Funding, and you'll receive..."

In Summary

Depending on the type of home you're attempting to sell, there are several creative ways to combine guerilla marketing techniques with classifieds, online classifieds or flyers to create an impact that will attract potential buyers. Zero down payment campaigns or low down payment campaigns attract buyers to ask for more information. A good voice mail system can capture the information of those potential buyers and help you to sort them into those that are likely to qualify and those that aren't, while helping to position you as an expert.

Loren Keim's Compelling Buyers to Call

Other enticing offers based on financing might include lease purchase offers, paying the buyer's closing costs or offering free job-loss protection or home warranties. These techniques tend to attract buyers who may not even be in the market to buy until they learn about your offer.

While it takes time and effort to investigate potential loan programs that will attract attention, to craft and test the ads on those programs, and to order and set up the voice mail system, it can be an effective method of attracting *many* potential buyers to contact you to purchase a home.

Chapter 9 – Sphere of Influence and Past Clients

Although I talk about Realtors using their sphere of influence to grow their business in every book I write, agents still argue with me, looking for the next great advertisement that will make them rich. We know that over half the homes you sell over your career will either be your sphere of influence, family, friends, old co-workers, ex-girlfriends, and past clients, or referrals from that group. Studies have repeated this for decades, yet we ignore this segment of our market because we think *"they know us"* and *"they'll call us when they want to buy or sell."*

This group can absolutely become your best source of leads. You probably know at least one hundred people that you see from time to time. Just look at the number of friends you have on Facebook without even trying. You have family, friends, old acquaintances, former co-workers, college roommates and even the doctor, dentist and hair dresser that you see on a regular basis. Each of these one hundred knows another fifty that you don't know. That's a potential pool of five thousand people you can tap into if you approach them correctly and train them to refer you to others who may want to buy or sell homes.

Loren Keim's Compelling Buyers to Call

Agents often don't realize that their 68 year old Uncle Charlie is in charge of a local veterans' benefits organization that could potentially refer you dozens of clients a year that can buy with little or no money down using their VA eligibility. Your Aunt Abigail is still in contact with her friend who is in charge of personnel at the local hospital that is bringing in new doctors from other parts of the country. Each of those doctors needs housing.

The truth is that every person you know has their own internal database of people they connect with regularly. This group of people is *their* sphere of influence. Your goal is to hopefully convince your sphere to use you in every real estate transaction, and also to leverage your relationships by tapping into *their* sphere of influence.

As your career grows, you'll add past clients, business associates and new contacts to this base of clients. In fact, according to the National Association of Realtors, 74% of clients will give you a referral if you keep in touch[x].

Almost twenty years ago, I met a man named Larry, who was living in a roach-infested tenement in Easton, Pennsylvania. This man referred me to clients who owned several hundred properties in Pennsylvania. You will never know who you can connect with until you start asking for help from those around you.

And please avoid saying, "*I don't need to send anything to my family and friends. They all <u>know</u> what I do.*" They really have no idea what you do. The truth is that as much as your Aunt Petunia likes you, at this point in your career, she's probably not going to refer you to her old high school boyfriend who is now President of the local bank.

Why? Unfortunately, Aunt Petunia, like all your relatives and friends, remembers you from your prior career or from when you were a child. She can't visualize the young man who got in trouble twenty years

Loren Keim's Compelling Buyers to Call

ago for drag racing in the neighborhood or the young lady who played with Barbies as a successful real estate professional and she doesn't want to hurt her present relationships by telling them about you because she doesn't understand how committed you are.

It's not that Aunt Petunia and Uncle Charlie don't love you. They do. But they are afraid that if you make a mistake, it will come back to haunt them. One of our most successful techniques at my firm has been to assist agents in appearing successful before they actually <u>are</u> successful. This technique involves keeping you in front of your sphere of influence, but also showing your sphere of influence some evidence of production.

In the next chapter, you'll be introduced to client databases. Suffice it to say that you'll need to create a list of all those people you have some contact with, and you need to store that information in a system that is easy to access and can help you contact many of them simultaneously. That's called a database. This information can be stored in a contact management software program like Top Producer or ACT.

Collect all the names, addresses, phone numbers and email addresses for everyone that knows you. Enter that information into a database program or contact

---

Sphere of Influence Prospecting

Step 1 – Compile a list of 100 acquaintances.

Step 2 – Get their addresses, phone numbers and email (if possible) and enter them into a database.

Step 3 – Write an initial letter explaining you're in Real Estate and need their help finding clients.

Step 4 – Follow up in 2 weeks with a "Properties for Sale" flyer.

Step 5 – Follow up in 2 more weeks with an "Evidence of Success" postcard.

Step 6 – Send everyone a personal handwritten note in the first 90 days.

Step 7 – Schedule ongoing mailings.

Loren Keim's Compelling Buyers to Call

management program. The key is to get a database put together quickly so that you can begin contacting the database consistently.

The next step is to outline a plan to convince them that you are the best person to call when anyone has a real estate question.

If you're brand new to the real estate business, you'll first need to announce that you have entered the exciting world of real estate. Then you need to send information that will convince your sphere that you are the "go-to" person for anyone needing assistance.

If you're an experienced Realtor, and have been selling for the last eight thousand years, you still need to visually show them what you do and how you do it.

We recommend that whether you are new or experienced, contact your sphere a minimum of six times during the first 90 days of your new re-connect with your sphere campaign. The six contacts does not include Facebook or other social media, but rather should be specific to your real estate career.

After your initial 90 days, you should follow up with your sphere at least once a month, if not more. Your initial letter should be simple and to the point.

For a New Agent:

Dear Aunt Petunia,

As you may know, I've made a career change. I'm now a licensed Real Estate Agent and I've affiliated with one of the top firms in Eastern Pennsylvania, Century 21 Keim Realtors.

Loren Keim's Compelling Buyers to Call

> In order to obtain my license, I had to take several courses over the past few months and a State Exam. To join Century 21 Keim, I've had to complete a lot of additional education, but I think it's all been worth it. Real Estate is an exciting business!
>
> I'm hoping you'll help support me in my new endeavor. If you hear of anyone thinking of buying or selling property, please call me. I'll include a few of my business cards with this letter. Please put them in your wallet or purse and give them out to anyone you can.
>
> Remember, although I may be new to the industry, I've had a lot of education and training, and I'm backed by some of the top people in Real Estate here at Century 21 Keim.
>
> Thanks!

For an Experienced Agent:

> Dear Aunt Petunia,
>
> As you probably know, I've been a professional Realtor in the area for the last 11 years and I'm affiliated with one of the top firms in Eastern Pennsylvania, Century 21 Keim Realtors.
>
> As challenging as the last few years have been, I've continued to grow my personal business and help home buyers to find great deals, home sellers to sell in the current market, and help investors to make smart buying decisions.
>
> I won't kid you, though. I could really use your help. If you hear of anyone thinking of buying or selling property, please call me. I'll

Loren Keim's Compelling Buyers to Call

> include a few of my business cards with this letter. Please put them in your wallet or purse and give them out to anyone you can.
>
> Remember, in a tough market, experience counts and I've been successfully selling real estate for a long time, and I'm backed by some of the top people in Real Estate here at Century 21 Keim.
>
> Thanks!

Your second letter should be "*evidence of your success*" with a reason for the recipient to contact you. In this case, evidence of success might be several listings for sale. That will show your sphere that you are actually working to sell properties. If you're new in the industry, it's unlikely you'll have any listings, so you'll need to "borrow" some.

You're going to send out a flyer that displays two or three different properties for sale, with your name and company name on the bottom of the flyer. You don't actually say anywhere that they are your listings, but your sphere of influence will assume they are, and their impression of you will hopefully shift. The reaction you're looking for is "*Wow, John seems to be doing well after only a few weeks*".

Ask around your office to find out if anyone would mind if you send copies of other agent's listings with your name on them to your clients. It's rare that an agent will tell you that they don't want you exposing their property to a few hundred people in your database.

Loren Keim's Compelling Buyers to Call

Do you know a buyer for any of these homes?

New Parkland Colonial! The Chesterfield in Rising Sun Farms. This fabulous home features 4 ample sized bedrooms, 4 full baths., 1st floor study with area for center family room with gas fireplace, custom Kitchen w/ Cherry cabinets & granite counter tops, Master retreat with sumptuous master bath . Upgrades incl: stone and stucco front, 3 car side entry garage, 42 inch kitchen cabinets, GE appliances, and more! $519,900

Saucon Valley Estates - Live in luxury! This newly painted 2 story colonial has hrdwd flrs throughout! 4 BRs, 2.5 Baths, mod eat-in kitchen, dining rm, living room, family room, finished full basement! Pellet stove in liv rm and fireplace in fam rm are sure to keep you warm and cozy! Family room walks out to back yard patio. Back yard is fenced in for privacy, and contains above ground pool, with newly refinished deck. $294,900.

Country Bi-Level - Beautiful Bi-Level with lots of room to roam. This 3 bedroom, 1.5 bath bi-level has everything you need. A new Florida room, a 2 car garage and a above ground pool all on a 1 acre lot. Priced at just $179,900

For More Information, Please call:
Loren & Theresa Keim
Century 21 Keim Realtors
800-648-4421

Your third mailing, done only two weeks after the second, should be a simple postcard with more evidence of success, but this time, it should be in "story" format. Again, each different story you mail to your sphere is likely to set off bells in the reader's mind of someone *they* know who is in the same situation. You're more likely to receive referrals if

Loren Keim's Compelling Buyers to Call

your sphere understands all the various aspects of your business. Tell them what you do with stories.

How I Helped Wanda and Greg Buy a Home Despite Past Credit Issues!

Wanda had medical problems and for more than a year, she was out of work. Greg simply couldn't pay the bills on his own and after six months of struggling, they had to give their car back to the bank and renegotiate their credit card payments. But now, Wanda and her husband were finally going to have a home of their own, and be able to stop throwing money away on rent each and every month. Wanda was thrilled with the new home she was able to buy with a loan program my team introduced her to this past month. She didn't realize that a home could be purchased with her credit situation.

At this point, you should begin sending personal notes to everyone you know. Purchase a few boxes of blank note cards from your local office supply store. Then set up a time each morning to write between five and ten personal handwritten notes. If you send out five each day, you'll get through all one hundred people in your database in just twenty work days. Your goal is to let them know you're thinking of them, and personally ask them for assistance. Obviously you can write to them on Facebook as well, but keep in mind that Aunt Petunia and Uncle Otto are not *on* Facebook.

One of the other surprising things I've discovered of top agents across the country is that almost all the top agents I've met follow a regiment of sitting down every morning between 7:30 and 9:00 and writing out between five and twenty personal handwritten notes. Personal notes really connect and resonate with people. If you plan to continue the practice after your initial wave of notes to your sphere of influence, you may have to really think hard each day of who you want to write to, but it will keep you in the forefront of many people's minds.

Loren Keim's Compelling Buyers to Call

Sample personal notes:

Hi!

　　I was just going through my files today, and realized how long it's been since I spoke with you! I love working with fun people like you...

Hi!

　　Thanks for considering using my services, it really means a lot to me...

Hi!

　　I was thinking about you today, so I thought I'd write you a quick note. I just wanted to say thanks for all the little things you do for others...

Hi!

　　I'm waiting for a client at the office today and have a few extra minutes. I thought I'd jot you a quick note.

　　Thanks so much for speaking with me

Loren Keim's Compelling Buyers to Call

Your fourth mailing might be similar to your second, with three homes on the flyer, but this time use three sold properties. The headline of this flyer could read *"Successful Sales by Our Team!"* and the tag line on the bottom of the flyer could say *"If you know of anyone thinking of selling a home, land or investment property, please have them contact me."* Again, even though you are honestly telling people that your firm sold the homes on the flyer; your sphere of influence will naturally read this to say that <u>you</u> just sold 3 homes.

This will lead to your family and friends talking about how well you're doing in your real estate profession. Again, your entire goal is to convince them that you are the person to refer, and this will typically do it. Build on your initial letters with similar marketing pieces over the first year. Keep in constant contact with this group, and add to the group continually as you meet new people.

Creating Your Sphere of Influence List

Anyone you know can be part of your sphere of influence list. That includes your family and friends, old acquaintances from work, school or life in general. Anyone you see on a regular basis, whether it's your doctor, hair dresser or the guy at the local pizza joint, should also be included on your list.

One way to grow the list over time is to ask permission to mail a few things to them. Tell them you'll be sending valuable information. This will help them to visualize you as a professional real estate agent rather than a client of theirs.

You: *"Hey, Becky, you are the best hair dresser in the entire Silicon Valley area. My hair looks great."*

Becky: *"Thanks."*

Loren Keim's Compelling Buyers to Call

You: *"No, thank you. By the way, I realize you see a lot of customers every week. You do know I'm in Real Estate, right?"*

Becky: *"Sure, I think you mentioned it."*

You: *"Well, we have a great program right now where we're sending out information on the market and sometimes some items of value to our best friends and customers. Would you mind if I added you to the list?"*

Becky: *"No, that's great."*

You: *"Should I use your address here at the salon, or send it to your home?"*

Memory Teasers

Over the next few pages are some memory teasers of people in different job professions. Glance through the list and try to think of anyone you might know or any past acquaintances that have these occupations. Then write them down, find their current mailing address and add them to your database!

Accountant	Interior Decorator
Actor / Actress	Janitor
Administrator	Jeweler
Aerobics Instructor	Jockey
Air Traffic Controller	Judge
Ambassador	Junk Dealer

Loren Keim's Compelling Buyers to Call

Amusement Park Worker	Karaoke Buddy
Anthropologist	Karate Trainer
Apartment Manager	Kitchen Cabinet Maker
Appraiser	Kitchen Installer
Archer	Lab Technician
Architect	Landscaper
Arms Merchant	Lawyer
Art Dealer	Librarian
Artist	Locksmith
Assembly Worker	Lumberjack
Assistant	Machinist
Astronomer	Magician
Astronaut	Maid
Auctioneer	Manicurist
Author	Marriage Counselor
Auto Mechanic	Mary Kay Rep
Auto Worker	Masseuse
Avon Lady	Mechanical Engineer
Backhoe Operator	Mercenary
Baggage Handler	Military Officer
Baker	Mobile Home Dealer
Banker	Mold Tester

Loren Keim's Compelling Buyers to Call

Barber	Mom
Bartender	Mortgage Officer
Beer Distributor	Mother-in-law
Bird Watcher	Mover (Beer Drinking Friend)
Book Dealer	Mover (Professional)
Bookkeeper	Musician
Bowling Buddy	New Car Salesperson
Brain Surgeon	Nightclub Performer
Bus Driver	Nightclub Owner
Business Executive	Novelist
Business Owner	Nudist
Butcher	Nurse
Butler	Nurses Aid
Cab Driver	Oil Delivery Guy
Car Pool Buddy	Ophthalmologist
Carpenter	Painter
Carpet Cleaner	Paramedic
Caterer	Party Planner
Chauffeur	Paving Contractor
Chef	Pediatrician
Chemical Engineer	Pharmacist
Chimney Sweep	Photojournalist

Loren Keim's Compelling Buyers to Call

Chiropractor	Physician
Civil Engineer	Physicist
Civil Servant	Pianist
Class Instructor	Pilot
Cleaning Person	Pizza Delivery Guy
Clown (Class)	Plastic Surgeon
Clown (Professional)	Plumber
College Professor	Podiatrist
Columnist	Police Officer
Computer Programmer	Politician (Corrupt)
Concierge	Politician (Honest)
Concrete Contractor	Postal Worker
Congressional Aide	Priest
Congressman	Printer
Congresswoman	Prison Guard
Construction Worker	Proctologist
Cosmetologist	Professional Athlete
Criminal	Psychiatrist
Dental Hygienist	Psychologist
Dentist	Psychotherapist
Dermatologist	Publisher
Detective	Radio Personality

Loren Keim's Compelling Buyers to Call

Developer	Rancher
Dietician	Receptionist
Drill Sergeant	Referee
Economist	Rental Agent
Electrical Engineer	Reporter
Electrician	Restaurant Owner
Entertainers (Adult)	Restaurant Server
Entertainers (Kids)	Rock Star
Executive	Roofer
Executive Secretary	Scientist
Exterminator	Security Guard
Factory Worker	Septic Inspector
Farm Hand	Sex Therapist
Farmer	Shoe Repairman
Fashion Designer	Social Worker
Firefighter	Song Writer
Fisherman	Sports Announcer
Fitness Trainer	Steel Worker
Flight Attendant	Stenographer
Florist	Stock Broker
Football Player	Stone Mason
Forest Ranger	Super Hero

Loren Keim's Compelling Buyers to Call

Funeral Director	Surveyor
Gardener	Tailor
General Contractor	Teachers (your kid's)
Golf Caddie	Teachers (yours)
Golf Pro	Telemarketer
Grocer	Termite Inspector
Gynecologist	Therapist
Hair Dresser	Train Conductor
Handyman	Travel Agent
Health Care Worker	Tree Surgeon
Heart Surgeon	Truck Driver
Home Inspector	Used Car Salesman
Hotel Owner	Veterinarian
House Wife	Wall Paper Hanger
Insurance Salesperson	Wedding Planner

In Summary

Although you'll discover many great ideas in this book to build your pool of buyers, do not underestimate the power of those people who already like and trust you. In the long run, your family, friends and past clients will refer you much of the business you need to earn a great income. Be certain that your sphere of influence knows exactly what you do and how they can assist you in building your personal real estate practice.

Loren Keim's Compelling Buyers to Call

Stay in contact with them, and deliver evidence of your success as well as specific requests for their help in finding customers. If you're not regularly keeping in touch with them currently, lay out a game plan and get to work showing them how they can help you.

Chapter 10 - Follow-Up Systems

What is one of the first things we are taught when we begin our real estate career? Follow Up, Follow Up, Follow Up. Yet we either very quickly forget it or we are afraid that we are 'bothering' the prospective clients. Follow-up is absolutely one of the most critical factors to our success in this industry, and in life.

Many years ago, while attending a graduation party for my friend's twin daughters, I met a young woman named Theresa. I liked the way she looked, the way she stood and during a long and interesting conversation with her, she mentioned that she was an office manager at a local personnel company and that she was taking real estate classes which meant that we had something in common.

At the end of the evening, I asked if she'd like to go out some time, eliciting the response that, although she was certain I would make a pleasant companion, she had recently broken off a relationship and wasn't looking for another one. She wanted some time to herself. I gracefully acknowledged the blow-off and pretended not to be hurt, but I couldn't stop thinking about her.

Loren Keim's Compelling Buyers to Call

The next day, I sent flowers to Theresa at the personnel company. She called and thanked me, but she said she really wasn't interested. I seemed like a nice guy, but the answer was still 'No.'

The following day, I once again sent her flowers. She called immediately and told me that she thought she had made her feelings plain. She was not interested. She would not go out with me and I should please stop bothering her. She finished the announcement by firmly saying "No *really* means no. It does not mean that I'm playing hard to get."

On the third day, my thick headed Irish side took over and I again sent her flowers. "I just want you to understand," she began on her call to me, "that I consider this stalking and possibly harassment. If it doesn't end, I may have to take action against you."

"Listen," I replied. "I won't send you flowers again. I promise. However, you told me that you are taking real estate classes. I don't know who you're planning to affiliate with, but whoever it is, it's a mistake, because my firm offers better training, better marketing, the best commission structure available and we even offer profit sharing. Is it possible for us to get together *just* to talk about your career path and what my firm can offer you? I promise not to ask you anything personal."

"That sounds fine," she said.

"Great, why don't we do it over dinner? I'll pick you up at six."

Ultimately, I married her. By the way, repeated contact is called follow-up. Over the years I've learned many life lessons. This experience taught me that the easy path is giving up. Success is earned by those who don't.

Once you receive a buyer call, you now have a prospect that has identified themselves as someone considering buying a property. You've

Loren Keim's Compelling Buyers to Call

hopefully received some sort of permission to call back. Now you need to follow up regularly. The average buyer speaks with between five and ten agents before purchasing. The agent who eventually sells a property to the prospect is often the agent who follows up most vigorously.

I'm not suggesting that you call the prospect every hour until they buy, but you need to maintain consistent contact. If you want to be in the bottom 95% of Realtors and be doomed to leave this industry in three years or less, then certainly you can do what everyone else does and follow up sporadically, inconsistently or not-at-all. If you want to be in the top 5%, you have to have consistent systems that you apply effectively to keep in touch with those potential clients who identify themselves.

Part of that contact can be emailing or mailing listings of properties, but part of it *must* be actual telephone or physical contact. Too many Realtors believe if they simply put a buyer on an automated email for listings, the buyer will come back when they find a home. The truth is that most of them are getting listings from multiple agents and they will work with the one who communicates with them directly. Sending listings to the prospect, however, *does* give you a reason to call.

Agent: "Hi, John? This is Malcolm at Greater-Than-Everybody-Else Realty. I sent you some listings yesterday. I just wanted to make sure you received them."

Client: "Yes, I did."

Agent: "That's great. Sometimes our emails get caught in people's spam filters. I just wanted to make sure they came through. Have you had a chance to look through them yet?"

Client: "No, not yet, but I saw the email."

Loren Keim's Compelling Buyers to Call

Agent: "Okay. I'll check back with you in a day or so. Let me know if any of the properties look interesting enough that you'd like to tour them."

Client: "I will."

In my firm, our buyer specialists keep in touch by setting aside one afternoon a week to call through all of their prospects. Buyers who are actively searching for property may need to be called every other day or even daily. You'll have to make a judgment call on each prospect.

I suggest separating your buyers into categories so you'll have an easier time creating follow-up routines or systems. As I mentioned way back in Chapter 3, you could start by separating buyers into A, B and C buyer categories.

As you start building follow-up systems, I would create separate ones for each type of buyer. If you're automatically staying in touch with buyers who want to buy but aren't yet ready (incubator buyers) or buyers who wish they could buy but believe now is not the right time for them (fence-sitter buyers), more of them will eventually become ready, willing and able anxious buyers and purchase a home from that person who maintained contact.

A word of caution, however, is that you don't want to waste your time actually showing lots of homes to buyers who are not ready, willing and able. Professional lookers will use us, abuse us and waste our time. As you work with more buyers, you'll have to learn the signs or clues that indicate what type of buyer you're working with.

Handling each type of buyer

1. **The Abuse-The-Realtor Buyer** - Because these buyers don't take us seriously and expect us to be available around the clock within

hours of them calling, we need to first determine if they are serious and qualified and second be certain to do a full buyer presentation to educate them on how we work and the value in our services. You must take the time to educate each of them, and they may become your best source of leads.

2. **Incubator Buyers:** You cannot afford to waste a lot of time showing them homes, so you should put them on an automated search program and automated follow-up emails and reports, which I'll outline in the next section. Keep in touch by phone at least once every two weeks. If their credit is very poor and they need a year to correct it, I'd be likely to keep in touch by phone only once a month.

3. **Fence-Sitter Buyers** - The difference between incubator buyers and fence-sitters is that fence-sitters can actually purchase a home now, but aren't convinced now is the time to buy. With these clients you should go through a full buyer presentation and then go through the material in the first chapter of this book as to why they should buy sooner rather than later. If they are still not convinced, make sure to keep them on automated updates and maintain contact each week.

4. **Professional Lookers:** Every once in a while these individuals will buy a home, but it isn't worth your time showing them fifty or sixty homes with the probability being low that they'll ultimately purchase. Befriend a few new agents that need the experience. Meet the lookers and give them a full buyer presentation, and explain that you work as a team with Sally, or whichever new agent you've set up to work with you. Sally will show them homes, and if they buy, you'll receive a referral fee.

Loren Keim's Compelling Buyers to Call

5. **Bottom Feeders:** Once you've discovered that you're dealing with someone who is going to consistently offer 25% to 50% below asking price, refer them to a newer agent. It gives great experience to the new agent, and perhaps you'll receive a referral fee, without all the time invested.

6. **Anxious Buyer** – They have called several Realtors by the time they called you. Give them a full buyer presentation and then keep in touch with them as much as possible without offending them. Twice a week will work in most cases.

7. **Relocation Buyers** – Contact must be consistent, but you can be overly aggressive if the buyers aren't coming in right away.

Elbert Hubbard was quoted as saying "How many a man has thrown up his hands at a time when a little more patience would have achieved success." Again, a powerful follow-up system can be instrumental in converting any potential buyers into purchasers and advocates of your personal real estate business.

Systems

One of the primary differences between successful mega-agents and everyone else is that mega-agents create systems into which they plug prospective clients that automatically facilitate follow up with those clients.

When I started my career in real estate, I created a simple follow-up system out of index cards. I would create a 3x5 or 4x6 index card on each client and simply call through them, writing down the results on a regular basis.

Loren Keim's Compelling Buyers to Call

The front of the card had the client information including name, address, phone number, a description of their real estate needs and other basic information. The back of the card had the dates I contacted them and the results of each conversation. If I had a client for a long period of time, I would end up stapling cards together.

The computer revolution and web based hosting has made the process much simpler. All the information you need to maintain contact with a client can be stored on your computer. Every follow-up contact can also be stored on your computer.

First, you need to start with two concepts that are often foreign to real estate associates. The first is creating a client database in a database program or contact management program. The second is sorting that database by contact types.

Client Databases

If you don't have your clients organized in some form of electronic database, you need to go get one as quickly as possible. This database may be an online program, such as Top Producer, or it may be a program you purchase and install in your computer, such as ACT.

Unless you have some sort of contact management software, you'll be trying to maintain contact with your clients by hand and will be less able to compete with those agents who are more computer savvy. Any contact management program will have a list of your clients, along with their contact information.

Your clients should be grouped into different categories. I have a rather large database, so I attempt to differentiate them in several ways.

Loren Keim's Compelling Buyers to Call

My primary distinction in groups is by a combination including the type of property and client. For example, some of the categories I use are:

- First Time Buyer - Anxious Buyer
- First Time Buyer - Fence Sitter
- Move-Up Buyer - Anxious Buyer
- Move-Up Buyer - Fence Sitter
- Horse Farm Buyer – Relocating
- Horse Farm Buyer – Local - Anxious
- Investor
- Past Client
- Sphere of Influence

You have to come up with a system that works for you that you understand. I use Top Producer, and strongly recommend the software. In my Top Producer database, I have contacts that have multiple contact types. For example, someone could be in my sphere of influence, but also be a move-up buyer who is anxious, or might be an investor.

These categories allow me to send targeted mailings or e-mailings just to the group that will value the mailings. For example, I send out several e-newsletters. One is targeted specifically at real estate investors. All my marketing to this group has a specific theme and includes free reports and a USP that targets that group. My sphere of influence, on the other hand, receives fun mailings that still include free reports, but a very different USP. Farm buyers and sellers make up another group that receive newsletters targeted at what's happening in the equestrian or farm communities and how they're being impacted, and offers reports that service that direct group.

Customers in multiple categories may receive a variety of mailing or e-mailing pieces from me.

Loren Keim's Compelling Buyers to Call

Drip Systems

Have you ever visited a cave or cavern and had the tour guide explain that stalactites and stalagmites are really just mineral deposits from water slowly dripping on one spot over time? Any good contact management program that you purchase and use effectively will accomplish the same task. Over time, you're planting seeds about yourself and your business.

Each time you drip on a client, or rather communicate with them, whether by mail, phone, e-mail or in person, will help to build your long-term relationship with that person you're contacting. The most important facet of the process is laying out a system and continuing to follow that system.

I've found that in my own business, when I become busy, I forget to send out mailers or newsletters and I fail to maintain that consistent contact with my database. My business slowly deflates like a balloon with a slow air leak. When I begin reconnecting with the database, I am reminding friends, relatives and past clients that I need their help, and leads re-appear, increasing my personal business.

The same is true if you talk to a buyer, show them a home or two, add them to an auto prospecting program and then forget them for a few weeks. When you eventually call them, they purchased at an open house or saw a home with a competitor. Have you had a FSBO meet with you and because you didn't follow up, they listed with someone else?

To avoid this up-and-down cycle, you should plan out any contact system for a minimum of ninety days of activities. Plan to use a mix of newsletters, e-mails and personal hand written notes, interspersed with phone calls, and schedule these activities for specific dates over the next ninety days.

Loren Keim's Compelling Buyers to Call

Obviously you can re-use the material for multiple categories of client. For example, some emails for buyers might talk about the process of buying a home, which would apply to all buyers. Other emails might talk about selling your home first, which would only apply to move-up buyers.

You might create between five and ten newsletters that include links back to your website. The newsletters may work for most buyers. Use these newsletters as a portion of your plan. Write all the newsletters at the same time, if possible, so you simply have to send them or put them in the mail with very little thought.

As you put each of these plans together, you are creating "action plans" to systematize your personal real estate business.

Creating Action Plans

A few years ago, Rick DeLuca, a real estate trainer and former broker from Reno, told me that the agents in his firm would not have achieved their high level of success if they hadn't had systems to plug each client into. If the client, for example, was a "For Sale By Owner," the agent might have a follow-up system to apply to them that would be consistent, leading to a fairly consistent result. If the client were a real estate investor that had called into the office, they would be put into a different follow-up system.

What Top Producer and other software programs allow you to do is to craft those follow-up systems so that applying them to a client helps to create a strong relationship with that client and generates predictable results.

Again, a key to success is communication through a mix of contact methods. Using a combination of postcards, emails containing

Loren Keim's Compelling Buyers to Call

links, letters, newsletters and personal contact is far more effective communication with your database than simply using a single method of maintaining contact.

In this book, I'll use Top Producer as my example, because I am most familiar with it and it is available to all real estate companies. Programs such as Top Producer allow the user to set up "Action Plans" or "Action Sequences" that keep an agent on-track and assist the agent in keeping in touch with their target audiences.

Action plans are predetermined timelines that can contain pre-written letters, emails, postcards and reminders to make phone calls. These action plans can be set up to utilize each of these forms of contact at certain intervals. An agent may select an action plan to apply to a particular client that may automatically send out emails at certain intervals, prompt the agent to print prewritten letters and envelopes, and remind the agent to make calls.

An example for a customer who may buy a home within the next sixty to ninety days might contain the following:

- Day 0 – The day the plan is applied, automatically email a note thanking the buyer for speaking with you and explaining the agent's Home Search automated system.
- Day 0 – Also add a note to the agent to remind them to put the buyer on the agent's Home Search or Auto Prospecting program.
- Day 1 – Remind the agent to make a follow up call to the buyer "Hi, I don't want to be a pest, but I just wanted to check that you received our initial email of homes for sale. Sometimes our client's spam filters block our emails. Did you receive them?"
- Day 3 – Automatic email of a letter outlining the choices in mortgage lenders and programs.

Loren Keim's Compelling Buyers to Call

- Day 6 – Remind the agent to call the client to find out if they've seen any listings they might want to schedule an appointment to view.
- Day 7 – Automatic email of a letter explaining buyer agency and why it's so critical to hire a buyer's agent.
- Day 10 – Agent newsletter is emailed
- Day 14 – Automatic email called "Know the Neighborhood" which explains why choosing the right location is just as important as choosing the right home
- Day 17 – Reminder for the agent to make a follow up phone call.
- Day 18 – Send out a personal hand written note.
- Day 20 - Automatic email of a letter outlining the value of home ownership versus the cost of renting.
- Day 25 – Print and mail a pre-created letter "Checklist Before You Buy"
- Day 26 – Automatic email of an "Evidence of Success" letter explaining how the agent assisted a family in buying a home.
- Day 30 – Automatic email of a letter called "Timing the Market"

While Top Producer comes with a plethora of pre-written emails and letters, I tend to write additional emails with a personal touch and build my action plans out of those emails. The key is to have everything done so you can simply plug a prospective client into a system and have the system follow-up and remind us of when we need to call.

Each subscriber to Top Producer has a dashboard with a list of the day's activities. If the activities include ten letters that need to be sent out, a simple click of the mouse allows the letters to be sent to the printer, followed by envelopes if you desire.

Loren Keim's Compelling Buyers to Call

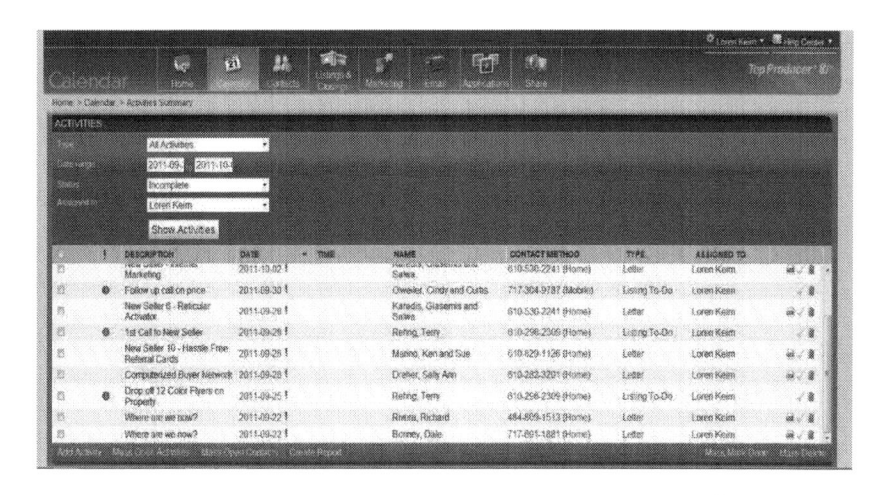

Below is a screen shot of some of Top Producer's action plans or campaigns which may provide a mix of contact methods with potential clients.

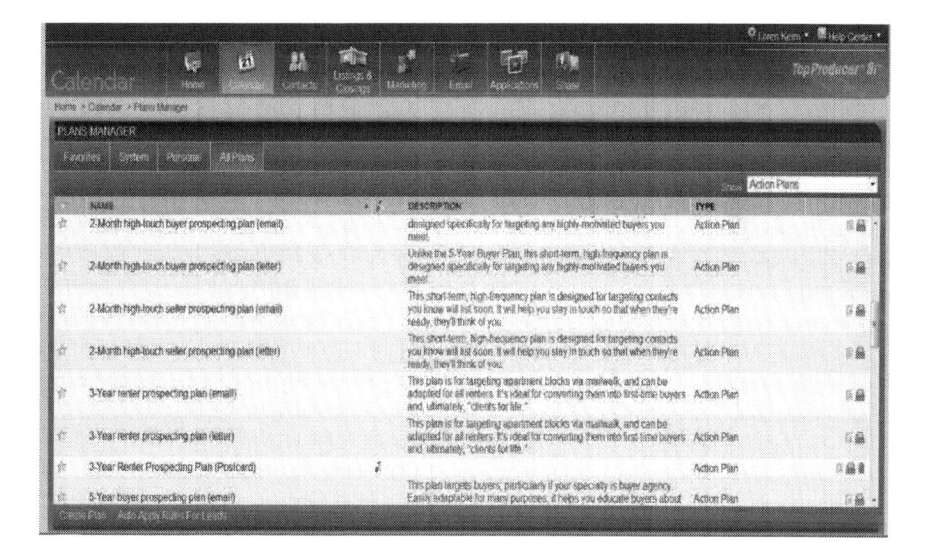

Loren Keim's Compelling Buyers to Call

ADDING TO YOUR DATABASE

Your income in real estate will be in proportion to the number of people you connect with regularly. Each time you come in contact with someone is an opportunity to build your sphere of influence and your database. As you meet people, whether in a real estate setting or in a social setting, you can ask them if you may keep in touch.

> Agent: *"Hey, it was great meeting you today. By the way, from time to time, I send my friends and clients information on the real estate market. Would you be interested in receiving it?"*

As I mentioned in the last chapter, this method can be used with your hair stylist, your auto mechanic, your doctor or anyone you see on a regular basis. This is a non-threatening approach to getting their permission to stay in touch. My experience is that most people will agree, and you'll be able to continually build your network.

Once you have a contact management system in place, adding potential customers allows you to easily send information to many individuals simultaneously, and in the case of email, virtually for free.

Auto Responders

Another form of follow-up system is what we refer to as "set it and forget it." You can fully automate your responses by using web software that connects to the consumer *for* you when a potential client fills out an online form. The program, or e-mail tool, that enables this is called an auto-responder.

There are some positives and negatives to using auto-responders. On the positive side, the client receives immediate gratification because typically they receive an email from you in seconds with the desired

Loren Keim's Compelling Buyers to Call

information. Auto-responders also can be configured to send ongoing information and keep you at top-of-mind awareness for the customer. Any good auto-responder software or service should also collect these email addresses for any additional marketing you would like to send.

One of the challenges of using auto-responders is that the client often realizes these emails are automatic and generic and therefore ignores them. This happens because there is typically only one auto-response system used for all the clients who make contact through a website, so they are all treated the same regardless of their ultimate needs and goals.

This is complicated by the fact that we've discovered many Realtors and mortgage originators who use auto-responders rely on them exclusively and fail to make any personal contact with the customer, which defeats part of the purpose of enticing a prospect to identify themselves as a potential client.

Again, this is often outweighed by the fact that the buyer receives immediate response, and can get that repeated and automatic follow-up that we are striving to create. Just be careful of how you implement the system.

Your first response might be an automated e-thank you note:

Hi John, I just received your request for information. I'll get that to you in a few minutes. I'm also going to send you a Consumer Notice that the state requires me to send to anyone who might buy or sell property with me.

Loren Keim's Compelling Buyers to Call

I do have a quick question or two that will help me to assist you with your goals. When are you planning to move? What areas are you considering and do you have a home to sell before you buy?

Again, I'll get you that information shortly and I truly hope I can assist you with your move!

Thanks again for contacting me!

Your auto-responder should immediately send a second email with any required Consumer Notices and a copy of whatever report was requested. After that, an auto-responder may work in the same manner as contact management software by sending regular emails that lead the potential client back to your site for more information or entice them to contact you for more details.

Humor

When designing action plans, remember that humor can be an ice breaker with your potential clients. For those of you who are skeptics and nay-sayers who believe that I'm being unprofessional even mentioning humor, let me pose a question. Which car insurance company comes to mind first when you want to save money on car insurance? It's also been more than a decade since we learned "Where's the beef?" But you know *exactly* where it is.

I've run ads like *"Loren Keim – Outstanding in his field"* with a photo of me in the middle of a farmer's field. Agents across the country run similar ads. Humorous messages you may have seen in your own marketplace include *"List your home with me, and I'll get right on it"* with a photo of the agent sitting on top of the house. I've seen several variations of ads that feature a Realtor sitting or kneeling next to their

Loren Keim's Compelling Buyers to Call

favorite dog. The captions all read something like: *"Trustworthy, Dependable and Loyal... and so is the dog."*

These ads and many like them have been run by Realtors across the country. Those Realtors who have the most success with comedic advertising tell us that the key is to make fun of yourself in a positive way. Self-deprecating humor, when done correctly, can evoke a strong positive emotional response.

However, when using humor, carefully analyze your audience. Messages that are too corny may generate a negative reaction depending on your target audience for the message. Additionally, make sure your message is not just humorous, but clearly indicates what you do and why you're exceptional. Too many agents believe that the humor alone will make a customer call. This can't be further from the truth. Every ad must have a clear and strong message associated with it.

In Geico commercials, the humorous tag line is *"I just saved a lot of money by switching to Geico."* The ad is funny and entertaining, yet the message is very strong, precise and clear.

A Final Word on Contact Management

If you don't yet have a contact management system in place, don't think about it – just do it. Go to my site, www.RealEstatesNextLevel.com and click on the link for Top Producer on the first page. We've negotiated a nice discount for you for purchasing this book.

Chapter 11 - Buyer Presentations – Step by Step

Why should you make a formal presentation to a buyer? Have you been bruised and abused by buyers? Have you ever had a buyer run you around the entire state only to purchase an open house from the agent sitting at that house or to purchase a FSBO directly from the owner? Do you really want to keep working that way? Perhaps this abuse gives you something to complain to your spouse about when you get home at night or to commiserate with other agents in the office by the coffee cart.

Formal visual presentations are critical when beginning your relationship with a potential client. Sadly, we only retain between ten and fifteen percent of what we hear, but we retain about half of what we see. As we learned in elementary school, showing rather than just telling is far more effective in communicating our message. Visual presentations might be done with a book, a flip-chart, a laptop with Powerpoint or an iPad.

Over the years, major real estate franchises have invested millions designing numerous books and flip-chart presentations that

Loren Keim's Compelling Buyers to Call

outline the buying process and the benefits of using an agent. While some agents feel more comfortable just talking to the buyer because they believe either showing a flip-chart or going through a Powerpoint is 'hokey,' I strongly recommend using any sort of visual presentation you can.

A simple method of creating a physical presentation is to purchase a three-ring binder and plastic sleeves. Use any word processor to create pages for each step of your presentation, print them and put them in the plastic sleeves, remembering to use photos or artwork on each page. The alternative is to create a presentation in Powerpoint.

Recently, Realtors have been putting their presentations on iPads or other tablet devices. The great news about tablet computers is that customers love them and are still enthralled with the devices. Pulling out a tablet and showing your Powerpoint on it captures their attention.

The Presentation

An effective buyer presentation should not only spell out why a Realtor has value to the buyer, but also show the buyer why they should refer you to their family and friends and can be used to really explain the process of buying so the client has a better understanding of the process.

Although there are many tasks we can accomplish with our buyer agency presentation, we have two primary goals during the presentation. First is to explain why they should work with you and second is to examine the process of buying, step by step and avoiding any pitfalls.

Whether you're building a physical flip-chart or a slide show on your tablet PC, start with a powerful statement to set the tone for the rest of your presentation. I prefer to set the tone by welcoming the buyer to our Preferred Buyer Service. My opening statement on my first slide is

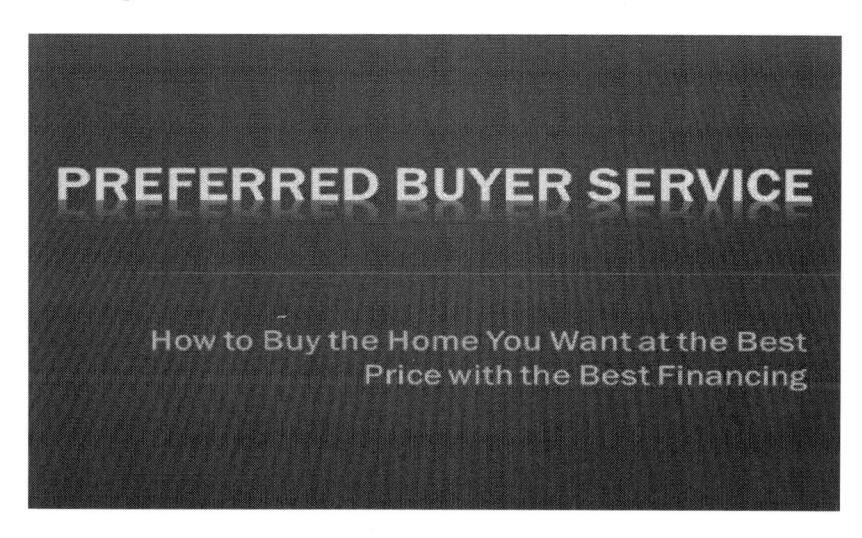

Loren Keim's Compelling Buyers to Call

"How to Buy the Home You Want at the Best Price with the Best Financing"

PREFERRED BUYER SERVICE

How to Buy the Home You Want at the Best Price with the Best Financing

Make your next slide or page specifically show the client your 'Unique Selling Proposition' for buyers. "I specialize in helping buyers to find their dream homes!"

I SPECIALIZE...

In helping buyers find their dream homes!

Loren Keim's Compelling Buyers to Call

Next, illustrate how you'll do more than simply show homes to a buyer. Your goal is really to assist them with the entire process.

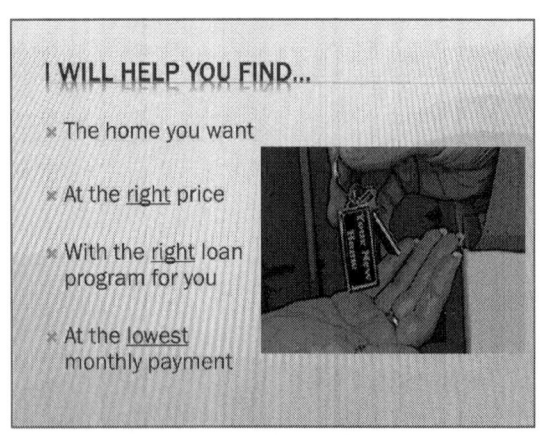

You're going to help them find the right home, but at a price the buyer can afford, with the loan program that best fits that buyer and the lowest monthly payment.

I WILL HELP YOU FIND...

- The home you want
- At the right price
- With the right loan program for you
- At the lowest monthly payment

By this point, the buyer is concerned that you're going to go into a two hour sales pitch, which they don't want to hear, and you're going to make them miss the big game featuring their favorite team this afternoon.

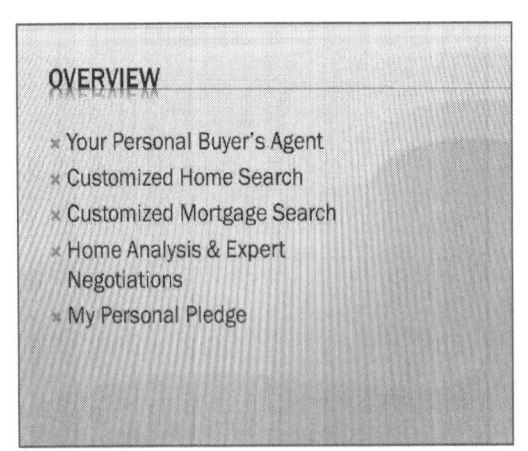

OVERVIEW

- Your Personal Buyer's Agent
- Customized Home Search
- Customized Mortgage Search
- Home Analysis & Expert Negotiations
- My Personal Pledge

If you've never heard of the Safe Island technique, it's the concept of alleviating anxiety by explaining in advance exactly what you're going to go over. Doctors utilize the same technique with patients to help calm them down by outlining how any medical procedure will work.

Explain that you're just going to spend ten minutes or so explaining how the process of buying a home works, why the buyer needs to be represented, how you work to find the best properties on the

Loren Keim's Compelling Buyers to Call

market, and the best mortgage products for the client, how you negotiate in their best interest and finally what you guarantee.

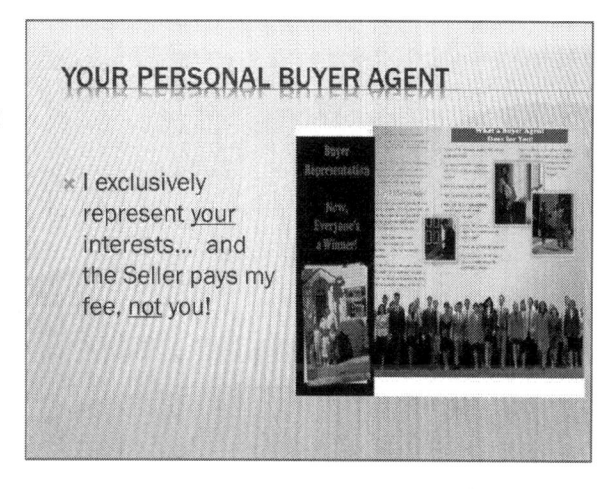

After giving a quick overview of what you'll discuss in your presentation, I tend to lead with what a buyer's agent is and is not. It is critically important to let the buyer know that if they are calling a dozen agents, in a false belief that more agents will find more homes, those agents may be working in the best interest of their home sellers and that you represent the buyer's interest exclusively. Better, the buyer pays you nothing.

At this point, I also explain that an agent is less likely to work hard for a buyer who does not commit to buy from them. This translates into the fact that talking to more agents actually does not help you find the best deals in the marketplace.

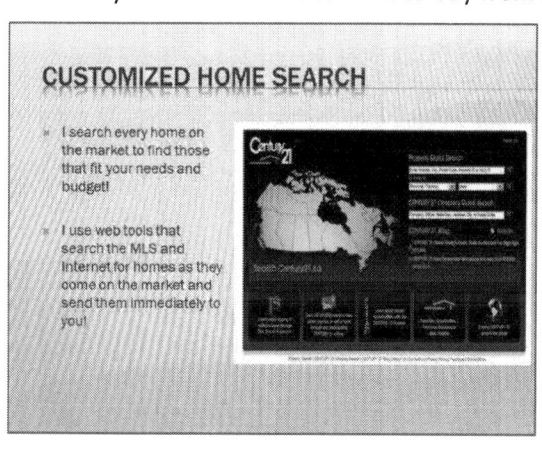

Take a few minutes and explain exactly how you use technology to search out the best values in the

Loren Keim's Compelling Buyers to Call

marketplace. If you use more than one multiple listing system, you might explain how that can benefit your search for the buyer's perfect home.

You might also include a slide or page that explains how you represent a buyer even if the seller is a FSBO and that you'll build your fee into the transaction.

The next section of my suggested presentation spells out how you'll assist the buyer in obtaining the best financing programs available.

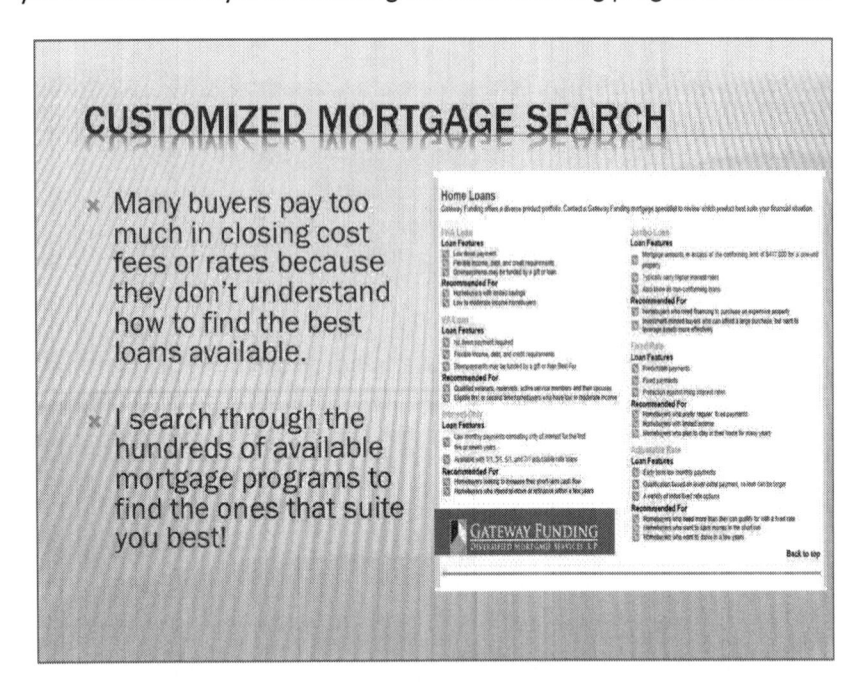

CUSTOMIZED MORTGAGE SEARCH

- Many buyers pay too much in closing cost fees or rates because they don't understand how to find the best loans available.

- I search through the hundreds of available mortgage programs to find the ones that suite you best!

Be conscious that you are a salesperson and the buyer does not have any strong reason to trust you at this point, so you have to carefully explain the benefit you receive from helping them. Be honest.

"Most Realtors are interested in getting you into a home quickly and they're familiar with typical loan programs like conventional bank mortgages and FHA loans. There are literally

Loren Keim's Compelling Buyers to Call

hundreds of loan programs however, offered by a variety of lenders. Some of these are low down payment loans and others are lower interest rates or better terms. Loans like Rural Housing Loans, first time home buyer programs and Community Reinvestment Loans are often ignored by most Realtors and lenders in favor of those they are most familiar with. My goal is to help you to find the best overall purchase, including the best loan program that fits your circumstances, your needs and your objectives. If I accomplish that, you might be so excited by my hard work that you might be more likely to refer me to your family and friends. Does that make sense?"

The statement "I want to find the best mortgage product and program for you" may be a significant challenge, however. There is a disconnect between doing our best to truly represent our buyer's interests and yet comply with the laws that require us to give many choices to our buyer for mortgage origination.

Have you ever had a buyer choose an online lender, because they thought they had secured a great interest rate, only to find that the money didn't show up at settlement? Or that settlement was postponed at the last minute by a week or a month or even that the closing costs were much higher than the borrower believed?

Although new RESPA regulations should hopefully correct the closing cost issue, being in the industry, we all know games that are played by some lenders to attract customers. The simple truth is that we *can*, if we want to represent our clients, find the best programs for them. We can search for programs by reputable lenders who quote accurate rates that don't change suddenly and that don't have lender junk fees attached.

Sadly, some Realtors will refer mortgages to their friends who do not necessarily have the best interests of the client at heart, which

Loren Keim's Compelling Buyers to Call

ultimately leads to RESPA regulations requiring us to step back from strongly referring one mortgage company or one mortgage program over another.

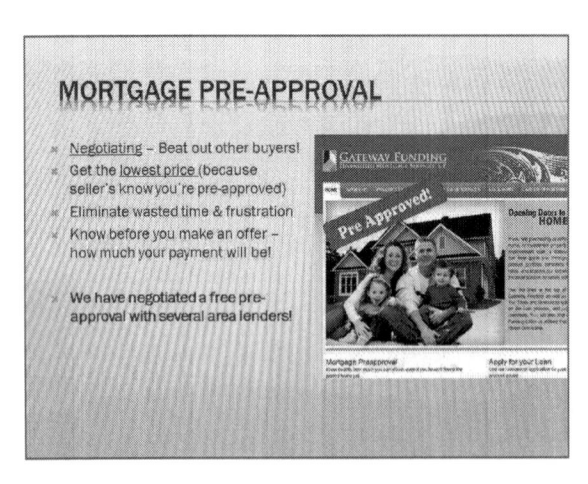

Explaining mortgages and the mortgage process leads to why a buyer should be pre-approved for a loan. We all know that if we're in a competitive situation, a pre-approval gives our buyers powerful leverage. We also know that a pre-approval saves our time and gas running around if the buyer can't obtain a mortgage or has a credit or income issue that has to be corrected before a mortgage approval. Another benefit for us is that a buyer who has a pre-approval that is coordinated by an agent is far less likely to go out and purchase from someone else.

Once you've explained how you'll assist the buyer in searching for the right home and how you can help them to choose the best loan program and get pre-approved for their purchase, take a few minutes and outline the process of purchasing a home. How do you set up appointments? How many homes should a buyer view in one evening or on one weekend? When they find the perfect home, do they need a deposit with the offer? What does an offer entail?

Explaining the process of purchasing is also taking a client out onto a safe island in order to minimize the fear a buyer has of making what may be the biggest financial decision of their lives.

Loren Keim's Compelling Buyers to Call

As you complete your explanation of the process of looking for a home, again highlight what you will do on the buyer's behalf. You'll be creating a market analysis of the property they want to purchase in order to offer a price that won't offend the seller, but will also be the best price for the buyer.

You'll be preparing the purchase offer and negotiating in the best interest of the buyer, again highlighting the difference between you and the seller's agent. You'll be attempting to roll closing costs into the purchase, if possible, negotiate the appliances and negotiate a home warranty if it's appropriate. You'll also then help the buyer coordinate their financing.

HOME ANALYSIS & EXPERT NEGOTIATIONS

AS YOUR REALTOR – I WILL...

- Perform a market analysis of your dream home.
- Use our right-price analysis to help suggest a reasonable offer
- Prepare your purchase offer
- Present your offer from a buyer's perspective
- Help you purchase the home at the lowest possible price.
- Negotiate to have the seller pay allowable closing costs
- Negotiate to have appliances included
- Negotiate to have repairs done by the seller
- Request a home warranty
- Coordinate financing with the lender
- Prepare and finalize paperwork for closing.

Buyer's remorse is a killer of real estate transactions. When the buyers leave your office, one turns to the other and says *"What did we just do?"* As I showed in Chapter One, I believe buying a home now and owning a home is a great investment for the long term. If you can convey

Loren Keim's Compelling Buyers to Call

that to a potential buyer, I believe you are helping them toward long-term retirement goals.

About a dozen years ago, I knew a real estate agent who, when he wrote an offer on a property, gave the buyers a huge horse pill in a clear plastic bag. The bag was labeled 'Buyer Remorse Pill.' It was a joke, but it would also open up a frank conversation with the buyer about the subject of buyer's remorse. One of the steps in bulletproofing any transaction is to have a discussion about all the possible pitfalls and create a plan to deal with them.

> "Mr. and Mrs. Weasley, after writing this offer, you will head home, and one of you will look at the other and say 'What did we just do?' You'll start worrying that you made an offer on the wrong house in the wrong neighborhood. Your furniture won't fit. You paid too much. You should have waited until the interest rates came down. You can't afford this mortgage payment and so on. If you get home and start feeling that way, don't worry. This is a common reaction called 'Buyer's Remorse.' Call me and we'll discuss it. Obviously you can and should talk to any professionals or experts you'd like, but I wouldn't let you do something that I didn't honestly believe was in your best interests."

The next part of your presentation should outline what happens after the offer is accepted, including the home inspection, any other inspections and the appraisal process. For the few of you readers who still avoid home inspections, and there are a few that argue with me about this, they are important for two reasons. First, you don't want your buyers to have some hidden defect appear after the transaction closes that could cost thousands of dollars. Secondly, you don't want the liability of a buyer suing you over a hidden defect.

Loren Keim's Compelling Buyers to Call

Obviously you should explain why inspections are so critical, but you should also carefully weave into your conversation the fact that home inspections often identify minor concerns that should not cause a transaction to fall apart. Improperly wired outlets and other easily correctable issues may be used by a buyer with buyer's remorse to back out when they get cold feet during the transaction.

If you believe home warranties are good investments for your buyers, you may want to include a page outlining the benefits of a home warranty and that you will try to negotiate for the seller to buy one. As home inspections help protect both the buyer and the Realtor, a home warranty may save us a lot of headaches later if something in the home unexpectedly fails.

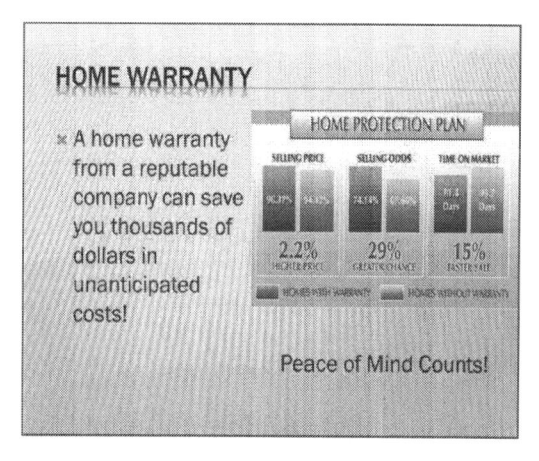

Loren Keim's Compelling Buyers to Call

Finally, point out that everything you do, including showing the buyer homes, finding them the best mortgage products, negotiating on their behalf, handling the paperwork and the inspections is all done at no charge to the buyer. You might also include a page that puts your promises in writing. Written service guarantees can be powerful motivation for a customer to be loyal to you.

Summary

Some real estate sales trainers tell us that we need to make sure every buyer comes to the office before we waste our time with them. I don't agree with that because I believe we throw away far too many buyers by failing to meet with them at least once. However, after that initial meeting you need to find a way to entice them to sit down for fifteen minutes so you can explain the way in which you work.

Some Realtors use a Consumer Notice as a crutch that they must go over agency relationships. It doesn't matter how you get the buyer to the point of listening to a formal presentation. It matters that you find a way to do it every time you work with a buyer. You must also use visuals so the buyer understands more of what you tell them and retains it.

Chapter 12 - Getting Referrals during the Process

Referrals are the lifeblood of our business. Every study I've seen on where actual closed sales come from indicates that more than half of our business is someone from our sphere of influence or a referral from a past client or our sphere of influence. Better, these customers often cost us little or nothing in comparison with all those we pick up from the thousands we spend in marketing homes for sale. More importantly, these customers often come to us pre-sold on our service by that person referring them to us.

Why do so many successful Realtors affiliate with large franchised real estate organizations? Some affiliate because of training or tools, but the vast majority joins these organizations because of name recognition. The most recognized real estate names give the agent instant credibility in the eyes of the customer and help to pre-sell the customer on using the agent's services. I am not suggesting, by the way, that you need to affiliate with a franchise or large independent to be successful. I am making a point.

Loren Keim's Compelling Buyers to Call

The principal of referrals follows the same logic. If one client loves your service enough to refer someone, you have instant credibility in the eyes of that referral.

Although I've spent the last two hundred pages outlining methods of attracting buyers, the simple truth is that we work to attract customers so that they will hopefully refer us more customers. The key is to make ourselves more referable and to proactively work toward generating those referrals.

The Reticular Activator

In his books, *The Psychology of Winning* and *The Seeds of Greatness*, Dr. Denis Waitley outlines many of the reasons we have to have clear and precise goals in our business and in our life[xi]. Being conscious of specific goals helps to activate a part of our brain that helps us to focus on those goals that we desire. This part of the brain is known as the reticular activator.

The reticular activator helps us to focus on those things that are important to us. As I pointed out several chapters ago, when we buy a new car, regardless of what make and model car you purchase, as you drive away from the dealer, you'll notice that same car virtually everywhere. It's almost like everyone went out and bought that same car the same day. That's because our mind focuses us on what is important to us.

This concept is critical to buyer referrals because home buyers are probably the group of people who are most tuned-in to other home buyers. When someone starts looking for a home, it seems like everyone else is looking too. Family and friends talk about it. Floyd in accounting mentions that he's looking as well. Within a few months of purchasing a home, this level of awareness tends to drop off.

Loren Keim's Compelling Buyers to Call

Please don't misunderstand me. We can generate referrals from clients for the rest of their lives if we act appropriately. As I pointed out earlier in the book, a National Association of Realtors study showed that 74% of clients will give you a referral if you keep in touch, but the buyer's laser focus on home buying is never more acute than during the purchasing process.

If we can find a way to hone this awareness into creating automatic referrals, our jobs become that much easier. Don't expect, however, simply to use magic words to obtain referrals. You have to be worthy of those referrals, and you have to be grateful to those who recommend you.

Letting Buyers Know We Need Their Help

While any good Realtor receives referrals from their clients, don't only rely on those accidental word-of-mouth referrals. Perhaps this sounds overly simplistic, but we need to make people aware that we need their help. You are actually costing yourself business when a friend or relative asks how the real estate business is going and you respond with *"Great! Never better. I am working seven days a week ten hours a day and have trouble finding time to go to the bathroom."* The last thing your friend wants to do is give you more stress when you're not seeing your family as it is.

A better response might be:

"I'm lucky that I'm as busy as I am in this market, but I'm always on the lookout for more business. If you run across anyone thinking of buying or selling, would you please recommend me?" You might even take it a step further by saying *"Actually, would you mind giving me a call and letting me know if you find anyone who needs help buying or selling?"*

Loren Keim's Compelling Buyers to Call

There are several key points in your relationship with the buyer when you can point out that you need their help and recommendations. The first is generally your buyer presentation. When you're laying out why you're going to do a great job for them, you can explain that most of your business is based on referrals from satisfied customers and you're hoping to do such a great job for them that they will recommend your service to others.

The second point is when you're writing an offer for the buyer. *"I'll work hard to get the best price and terms for you on this property, John and Sally. As I mentioned when we first met, most of my business is by referral, so I really want to do the best job possible for you so you'll consider recommending me to your friends and family."*

When the offer is accepted, you can again outline the next few steps in the process, which helps alleviate anxiety, and ask once again for their assistance. *"Well, Peter, we got the house. This isn't over, though, until we get to settlement. We have our pre-approval, but we still have to get through the inspection process and the appraisal. I'm sure they'll be fine, but I want to re-iterate that home inspectors are trained to create laundry lists of what may be minor repairs on the home. We'll have to carefully examine the report when it's done to see what we might want the owner to correct. Oh, and one other thing, since we found you a great home, I have some additional time to take on more buyers. Who do you know that is looking to buy a home but isn't yet locked into one particular agent?"*

The final point is at closing. The buyer is usually excited by their purchase and anxious to move in. They thank you for all your hard work. This is the opportunity to be more specific in your request for referrals. *"I'm so glad you're happy with your new home and hopefully the process wasn't too painful. Who do you know that I might help in finding the perfect home?"*

Loren Keim's Compelling Buyers to Call

Third Party Endorsements

One of the most powerful methods of building referrals is when our clients hear a third-party endorsement of our work. I first learned this when Paul, a mortgage originator with a local lender, started selling me to the clients I referred to him.

After an initial buyer agency presentation, I would try to set up a mortgage pre-approval appointment for each buyer. Again, a pre-approval helps to tie the buyer to us and shows the buyer that we are trying to do what is in their best interests rather than just showing them home.

When the buyer would meet with Paul, he would begin by introducing himself and say something like *"You were referred to me by Loren Keim. That gives me a double responsibility. I, of course, want to do a great job for you by getting you the best mortgage program available with the least amount of pain and discomfort, but I also want to do a great job for the Realtor who referred you to me. By the way, I don't know if you realize it, but Loren is one of the most successful Realtors in our area. The reason he's so successful is that he works harder than anyone to help buyers get to their dreams. You are really lucky to be working with him. In fact, if you have any friends or relatives who want to buy, don't let them get stuck with some other agent. Tell them to call Loren. He really cares about his clients."*

You may not be able to entice your lender to say all that, but I assure you that every person I referred to Paul that bought a property also referred me a client during the process. Sadly, Paul relocated to Idaho to be closer to family. I am not suggesting that you orchestrate a fake speech by your mortgage person, but I am saying you should share with them the fact that they can help you to generate more buyers who will, in turn, need mortgages. If they truly believe you are one of the best in the business and truly believe you will do more to assist clients than the next person, perhaps they will consider giving you a third party endorsement.

The same might be said for home inspectors, escrow agents, title agents or any other third parties that you refer to a buyer. Remind those businesses that share your customers that there are Realtors who charge additional buyer fees that you do not and that don't take the time to really listen to buyers and help them like you do. What is in the best interest of the buyer? Should they work with Realtors who really care, or with someone who is in it to make the quick sale and move on?

Referrals from Exceptional Service

In the book *Raving Fans,* Ken Blanchard outlines the concept that delivering service beyond a customer's expectation is a strategic advantage and can lead to clients who will actively refer your business for the rest of their lives. These clients are so excited about your business that they can't wait to tell others about what you did compared to your competition. They are raving fans of your business.

When clients are pleasantly surprised by the service you provide, and thank you for that service, it creates the perfect opportunity to ask for referrals.

Client: "Thank you so much for going the extra mile to negotiate those repairs."

Agent: "That's my job, and I'm happy to do it. And by the way, I'll do the same for any friends or co-workers of yours who might also need help in purchasing. Who do you know who might be buying a home over the next few months?"

Loren Keim's Compelling Buyers to Call

What steps can you take to set yourself apart from your competition and visually show your customers that you truly understand their needs and you care about them? While I can give you examples of some of the steps my team has taken, you should sit down with other agents in your organization and look at the entire purchasing process in your area. At what points might you be able to do something that is truly unexpected for the buyer?

Keeping in Touch

While this may seem like a no-brainer, I am continually surprised by agents who don't maintain proper contact after they write an offer for a buyer. You should be following up with the buyer's mortgage company every week and calling the buyer with an update every single week.

Staying in touch shows the buyer that you care about them and you're on top of any situation that might arise. Finding out about issues early also allows you to effectively deal with them and move forward.

Balloons and Coffee Mugs

Most buyers fully expect that their loan will be approved, yet they still have a nagging feeling of doubt. What if something unexpected comes up? What if all those ads on the radio about identity theft come true and someone ruined their credit? Buyers are still relieved when the final mortgage commitment comes through.

We have turned the mortgage approval into an event. The mortgage bankers we most often work with know that they are not to call the buyers when the mortgage is approved. That is part of our job.

When possible, we pick up five or six balloons and a coffee mug filled with candy kisses and head to the buyer's workplace. The relief they feel when they learn they are approved creates a positive mood and

Loren Keim's Compelling Buyers to Call

you are there to share that experience with your buyer. This emotionally ties the buyer to you. We have also found that buyers will typically take the Realtor around their office and introduce the agent as 'the best Realtor in the world.'

The cost for a few balloons, a coffee mug and candy kisses is less than ten dollars and is likely to create referrals. You might also have special coffee mugs made with your name and company on them. "Congratulations from Peter Parker at the Web Real Estate Agency." The mug is likely to sit on their desk as a reminder for the next few years and can be purchased personalized for only a few dollars each. Again, check out www.GideonPromotionalProducts.com for some examples.

Grocery Store Boxes

We contact local grocery stores to ask if they have any extra boxes from deliveries. Often we're able to collect these boxes, flatten and store them, and then drop them off at the homes or apartments of our buyers. Buyers really appreciate receiving extra boxes for their move, and they further appreciate that you took the time to go above and beyond.

Buyers will go to work or family parties and let everyone know that *their* Realtor dropped off boxes to help their move. Everyone else's Realtor vanished from sight as soon as the contracts were signed.

Thanking Your Customer

If you want more referrals, reward the behavior. That doesn't mean you have to send lavish gifts to the referring party. In fact, in many parts of the world it is against the law to give a gift that may be construed as paying a referral fee to an unlicensed individual. Someone's ego and self-worth is just as important as any gift. You can reward their behavior with praise, adulation and sincere thanks.

When a customer is referred to you, make a point of immediately calling the person who recommended your service. Tell them how much you appreciate their trust in your abilities and make the promise that you will do your best to continue to earn that trust by doing the best job possible for the person they referred.

You should then take a few minutes and write out a personal thank you card which explains that you appreciate every referral and you don't take lightly the fact that they referred you this client. You might also send along one of those coffee mugs from the last section with some candy in it.

A last important point is that you should then keep in touch with the client who referred you, because you want to show them that you are working hard to help. Keeping them in the loop goes a long way to garnering a second, third and fifteenth referral from that same client.

After sale follow up

When you close on a transaction, send an immediate thank you card to the buyer. You really appreciated them working with you and can't thank them enough. You hope they are happy with their new home, and please call if they have any issues or concerns. Additionally, if they have any family, friends or co-workers who need assistance, please let them know you'll be happy to help.

Step two is to plug these clients into a follow-up system, as we described in Chapter 9. You should have pre-written letters for thirty days, ninety days, six months and one year after the home closes. Each

Loren Keim's Compelling Buyers to Call

milestone is marked with a note that is automatically generated. Top Producer comes with follow-up letters like these pre-loaded.

The clients should also be receiving everything you're sending to your sphere of influence including newsletters, e-newsletters, evidence of success mailings and anything else. Your past clients are now part of your sphere of influence and should be treated as such.

Some Final Thoughts - Change is Inevitable

Remember our conversation earlier about the book *Who Moved My Cheese*. Change is inevitable. We can try to ignore it, hoping it won't happen. We can change when there is nothing left to do and participate in it. Or we can try to assess what is coming and get out in front of the pack and lead the change.

Over the next few years, we know more buyers will use handheld devices rather than desktops to search for a home. The iPhone, Droid and iPad revolution is already here. This change means that we have to adapt our technology tools to the devices our customers are using. We need websites that are friendly to handheld devices.

Search tools that allow you to click one button and have your phone geo-located, pulling up full information on any house you may be sitting in front of, is already available. What will we see next? Will buyers actually want to scan QR codes on real estate signs? I doubt it, but it's possible.

Knowing there is change means that we should be actively looking for tools that might benefit our buyers and might put us on top of the pack when competing for those buyers.

Loren Keim's Compelling Buyers to Call

Treating your Business LIKE a Business

Too often we forget that we *are* our own businesses within a business. While you may work for a real estate broker and be part of a national franchise or an independent organization, you are still your own micro-firm. Your income is going to be directly related to what you put into your personal real estate practice.

Every moderate sized firm has a top producer or a few top producers and a lot of agents that are struggling. Some statistics indicate that the typical real estate agent only survives between one and three years in the industry before giving up to get a 'real job.' The dirty secret is that there is nothing special about those who succeed in this industry. It is what they do that sets them apart from the vast majority of agents.

In the beginning of this book, I explained that the problem is *you*. In every part of the country, every single week of the year, good economy or poor economy, there are Realtors selling homes. This is true even in Las Vegas, Orlando and Miami. My vision for you is that you will be one of those agents that not just survives but thrives, becoming one of the top agents in your region.

Go to work each and every day with the expectation that you have to generate leads, follow-up with those leads, and deliver exceptional service to your customers so they refer you more customers. If you can create and maintain that focus, you will succeed!

Loren Keim's Compelling Buyers to Call

Index

A, B and C Buyers, 44
ACT, 195
Activerain, 123
ActiveRain, 141
Advertisement Calls, 61
Attraction Techniques, 68
Automatic Listing Updates, 83
Auto-Responders, 202
Balloons, 225
Broker Agent Social, 13
BrokerAgentSocial, 142
Business Cards, 112
Buyer Agent, 211
Buyers
    Abuse the Realtor Buyers, 45, 192
    Anxious Buyers, 46, 194
    Bottom Feeders, 45, 194
    Fence Sitter Buyers, 45, 193
    Incubator Buyers, 45, 193
    Professional Lookers, 45, 193
    Relocation Buyers, 46, 194
Buyer's Remorse, 215
Cartus, 92
Channels, 142
Classified Campaign, 162
Comparison USP, 97
Compelling Offers, 65
Contact Management Program, 195
Craigslist, 35, 165
Database, 195
Demographic Groups, 92

Denis Waitley, 220
Drip Systems, 197
E-mail, 110
Emotional Response, 104
Employee Relocation Council, 92
equestrian properties, 89
Evidence of Success, 107
Facebook, 123, 126
Federal Reserve, 18
First Time Buyers, 91
Flip-chart, 207
For Sale By Owners, 91
Fortune Cookies, 114
FourSquare, 143
Free Reports, 72, 78
FrontDoor, 36
Gerry Ballinger, 66
Gideon Promotional Products, 113
GoogleBuzz, 143
Green Homes, 93
Grocery Store Boxes, 226
Guerilla Marketing, 88
Hidden Defects, 216
historic homes, 89
Historic Homes, 88, 93
Home Inspection, 216
Home Search, 212
Home Warranty, 217
Horse Property, 93
Houselogic, 131
IDX feed, 31

Loren Keim's Compelling Buyers to Call

Image advertising, 52
Individual Property Advertising, 54
Inflation, 19
Interest rates, 20
Internet Calls, 63
Investment Property, 92
iPad, 207
Jay Abraham, 66, 89
Joe Stumpf, 66
Just Listed, 104
Just Sold, 104
Just Sold Prospecting, 91
Letters VS Postcards, 103
Life Events, 91
LinkedIn, 123, 139, 140
ListHub, 35
Mailers, 102
Malcolm Gladwell, 15
Market Evaluations, 81
Marketing Warfare, 88
Mortgage Approval, 225
Mortgage Bankers, 225
Mortgage Pre-Approval, 214
Mortgage Process, 214
MySpace, 123, 143
Newsletters, 109
Newsworthy Marketing, 71
Niche Market, 95
Niche Websites, 116
Performance Guarantee, 97
personal notes, 179
Personal notes, 178
Personnel Departments, 93
Point2Agent, 36
Postlets, 33

Preferred Buyer Service, 208
Promotional Items, 112
Promotional Products, 112
Prudential, 92
Rainmaker Niche Sites, 118
Real Estate Bubble, 41
Referrals, 226
Reticular Activator, 220
Senior Communities, 94
Short Term Prospecting Markets, 91
Sign Calls, 58
Smartphones, 143
Social Media Platforms, 123
Spencer Johnson, 41
Sphere of Influence, 92, 180
Squidoo, 123
Switching, 56
Syndicating, 32
Tablet PC, 208
Target Market, 87
Targeted Web Sites, 116
Testimonials, 107
The Tipping Point, 15
Third Party Endorsements, 223
Third Party Relocation Companies, 92
Top Producer, 199
  Market Snapshot, 82
Top Producer Software, 195
Traditional Buyer Business, 42
Trulia, 36
Twitter, 123, 137
Unique Selling Proposition, 94, 95
Unique Service, 96

Loren Keim's Compelling Buyers to Call

Viral Video, 144
Virtual Office Website, 31
Visual Presentations, 207
Who Moved My Cheese, 41

Yahoo Real Estate, 33, 36
Yellow Signs, 161
YouTube, 143
Zillow, 33, 36, 81

Excerpt from Loren Keim's
Life Lessons... from the Back Seat of My Car

(Available now)

Loren Keim's Compelling Buyers to Call

> *Life Lesson:*
>
> *We should always listen to the advice of others and carefully consider the opinions of those who know more than we.*

The Eldorado and the police...

About twenty years ago, when I was just beginning in real estate, I had invited friends of mine who were thinking of investing in property to my house for dinner, along with my girlfriend, after which we drove in my car, a big Cadillac Eldorado, over to the office to go through the Multiple Listing System. By the time we were finished, it was quite late, and none of us were particularly pleased when, having piled back into my car, we discovered that it would not start. So I called one of the most important emergency services in the country. Yes, I called AAA.

The tow truck driver, who was dispatched in response to my panicked call, looked over the car and announced that he *could* get the car started but it wouldn't make it very far. Even though he explained the problem, I was sufficiently mechanically challenged, not to understand it precisely. But the point is that, being young, macho and just plain stupid, I decided that since it was only a few miles to my house, where everyone had left their cars, I would make a run for it. And since the mechanic had told us that we had an electrical issue, I felt it would be better to drive with no

Loren Keim's Compelling Buyers to Call

headlights, and therefore we should stay off the major highway and just take the surface streets.

So, slightly after midnight on a Friday evening, I drove at a relatively high speed down Hamilton Street to Hanover Avenue in Allentown and took a short cut through a parking lot to try and save as much time as humanly possible, in the process of which I passed a police car going the opposite direction. I suppose it should have come as no surprise to me that the police cruiser spun around and, with sirens and lights flashing, proceeded to pursue me.

Making a quick turn around the corner, I pulled over leaving the car in park, naively assuming that I could simply explain to the officer why I was driving with no headlights and that he would certainly let me go the last mile to my home. As I went to open the big door of the Eldorado I noticed a police car pull up next to me in addition to the one that was now behind me, and another car approached from the other direction pulling up in front of my car, boxing me in.

Putting the car in park, and starting to get out, I turned to my companion, and over the noise of the loud engine said, "Keep your foot on the gas pedal, we're going to have to get out of here quickly". In the process of stepping out of the car, I somehow managed to trip over my own foot and land flat on the ground at one of the officer's feet.

To add a bit more context to this story, I should probably inform you, that having all but cut off my middle finger several weeks before by slamming it in the car door, the doctor at the Muhlenberg Hospital Center who had sewed me back together, had

Loren Keim's Compelling Buyers to Call

cast it with a metal bar on either side of my middle finger. As near as I can determine using hindsight, the police officers, seeing me take a dive with a metal object in my hand, assumed that I was armed.

Suddenly officers were diving behind their cars, drawing their guns as they did so. "Lie face down!" someone shouted. "And push that weapon away from you!"

I, of course, had no idea what they were talking about. After all, my only problem was that my headlights weren't functioning. So naturally, I stood up and said, "What are you talking about?"

And then, since they were all shouting at once, I got back in the car and shut the door, only to find myself caught up in a spotlight. Needless to say, when all of us were forced to get out of the car while the officers searched it, my friends and potential clients, not to mention my girlfriend, were far from pleased.

As it turned out, the police had been responding to the burglary alarm at a bank in the shopping center parking lot when they found themselves being passed by a large car with no headlights, with the result that they had pursued the car. Needless to say, they were extremely unhappy with this turn of events. Having bigger fish to fry, they eventually let me go.

The next day the five of us were at McDonald's on Union Boulevard in East Allentown with a group of probably fifteen other friends, busy recounting the story of what happened the night before. My friend Tom was in the process of making a few well chosen disparaging remarks about the incompetence of police

Loren Keim's Compelling Buyers to Call

officers in general, and one in particular, when he realized the rest of us were staring at him wide-eyed, and turning he saw the gentleman in question standing right behind him, arms folded across his chest and an unpleasant expression in his eyes.

I had never before seen someone actually faint.

Hidden in the Attic...

During the course of the last decade, most real estate companies conducted so-called caravans, by which I mean that all the realtors in any given office inspect all the new listings that have come on the market over the prior seven days, in order to acquaint them with the company's current inventory. Many companies still do this although, in my opinion, it's a wasted effort since the agents could be more usefully employed actually marketing the available homes.

> *Life Lesson: If someone doesn't want you to visit... there might be a good reason!*

Consequently, we stopped this practice a long time ago, replacing it with broker's open houses for unique properties.

In any event, several years before, one of our agents, Christa Klein, had brought in a listing of an all brick split level in the west end of Allentown, a beautiful house that we scheduled first on our caravan tour that coming Tuesday.

Loren Keim's Compelling Buyers to Call

As always, our receptionist called the owners to verify the Tuesday morning appointment to view the home. When Tuesday came, we joined two dozen other realtors at the house. I rang the doorbell and received no response, which was odd because the owner had definitely said that she'd be home. After knocking loudly and again, received no response, I decided to use the lock box on the front door. I had just begun spinning the dials when the door flew open.

The woman answering the door, presumably the owner, looked dumbfounded at seeing such a large group of people assembled in her front yard. "What are you doing here?" she asked, whereupon Christa took the lead, explaining that we were caravanning new listings and we were going to take a quick walk through the house just to get a look at the general layout.

But, she protested, the house was dirty. Couldn't we come tomorrow instead? And when I explained that Tuesday was our day to do caravans, and went on to assure her that we would look past the grime, she protested that she had dishes in the sink. And when I told her that would not be a problem, she told us that she'd be right back and shut the door, only to reappear a few minutes later and lead us down to the basement, muttering something about giving her time to straighten up a little.

This was early in my career and most of our office was made up of women, so I was attempting to show off my vast knowledge, having just completed a construction course, and believing I actually knew something about it. As a consequence, I was busy explaining the type of electrical service in the house and the size of

Loren Keim's Compelling Buyers to Call

the beams when the owner reappeared and told us we could go through the rest of the home.

We stepped up into the family room and looked around, and then proceeded to the next level to look at the dining room and kitchen. There were a good many dishes in the sink in the kitchen, but certainly that didn't detract from the nice oak cabinets and solid surface countertops.

Finally, we proceeded to the upper level and looked last at the master bedroom, which had its own bathroom and a walk in closet in which there was a trap door that allows access to the storage area of an attic.

Since there was a chair positioned directly underneath the trap door, I suggested that we take a look at the attic insulation and at the same time find out how much room there was for storage. But when I raised the door, I was surprised to find myself face to face with a pair of men's bare legs, and looking up, saw that the gentleman in question was outfitted in nothing but boxer shorts.

"I'm working on the attic fan," he said in a singularly unconvincing way, hoping no doubt to put us off.

But realtors are a curious bunch, and in the end every single member of my office staff wanted to also climb up on the chair and look at the man in the attic. This took about fifteen minutes. When we returned to the kitchen, we found our hostess pacing back and forth, wringing her hands. Then, pulling herself together with an obvious effort, she explained that the man in the attic was there to help her pack.

Excerpt from Life Lessons

Loren Keim's Compelling Buyers to Call

We later learned that the owner had been transferred to Texas where he had already started working while his wife remained at home to oversee the sale of the house. The sad part of the tale is that the husband called us two days later and told us he wanted the house removed from the market, because, he said, his wife was unhappy about the way we were "servicing" the property.

Needless to say, we failed to mention the man in the attic which she was apparently "servicing" very well.

> *Life Lesson: Investigate each situation before taking action. Don't rush in without all information.*

Selling a home at a busy intersection...

Some of the unwise things that home owners say when they're trying to sell their home constantly amaze me. Sellers, being emotionally invested in their property, are often their own worst enemy, making statements that absolutely cost them a sale.

As an example, a few years ago, I had a young couple named Stacey and Dennis, looking at a property along a very busy road near Whitehall, Pennsylvania for the third time, a house that was located at least a hundred feet off the road, behind a line of trees, but was only one door off a major intersection. The layout reminded Stacey of her grandmother's home, and she also appreciated the convenience of being very close to a major

Loren Keim's Compelling Buyers to Call

shopping district. Dennis loved the convenience of the home's proximity to his work, just five minutes away. Neither was bothered by the noise from the busy intersection, which apparently, was the primary complaint of potential buyers who had looked at the house previously.

As we were about to leave for the office to write up an offer, the seller pulled into the drive, and hurried out of his car towards us. "Wait a minute, wait a minute," he yelled, waving his arms. "Come back to the house. I want to show you something."

Given the circumstances, I could scarcely refuse, and in a few minutes we were standing in his living room.

"Do you hear that?" He demanded triumphantly, shutting the solid oak front door.

"Hear what?" I said.

"Nothing! That's exactly what I mean. You don't hear anything once that door is shut. There's no sound whatsoever. This house is so well built that you don't hear noise when the door is shut."

Assuring him that that was wonderful, I began to shepherd my buyers back outside.

"You don't understand!" he said, positioning himself between us and the door. It's really, really quiet in here. You can sleep without having to worry about being awakened by the noise."

Loren Keim's Compelling Buyers to Call

"Uh, okay." I replied, displaying my command of witty repartee. His emphasis on "the noise" was beginning to unnerve me.

"As a matter of fact," he continued, "there's a major accident every single week at the corner down there, and sometimes we don't even hear the sirens."

It was beginning to be perfectly clear to me that if I allowed him to continue in this vein, he was going to jinx the sale.

"Okay, that's fine. I'm sure the buyers appreciate that".

"You know, there are ambulances and police on this corner all the time because of the accidents," he confessed enthusiastically. "And we don't even hear the sirens. That's how well built this house is."

"That's wonderful. Thanks for your time," I responded once again.

He put his hand out, frantic that we were trying again to leave. "No, no, no, you really don't understand," he said. "For example, my son's best friend was killed on our front lawn last year. He was pulling out of our driveway and got T-boned on the main road right out there." He pointed behind him toward the front door. "His car rolled over into our front lawn. We had ambulance, fire trucks, and police in our front lawn with lights going, and sirens flaring, and we didn't hear a thing. That's how incredibly well built this house is."

My buyers and I were flabbergasted. Looking back at Stacey, I saw that her mouth had formed a perfect "O", which was

Excerpt from Life Lessons

Loren Keim's Compelling Buyers to Call

not surprising, given what she had just heard. On the way back to the office, her husband said, "Well, if we purchase the home, we'd have to buy a really big shop vac to suck the blood out of the front yard, won't we?"

It came as no surprise to me when they decided not to make an offer on the house which, eventually, sold for significantly less than the original asking price.

Sellers have to be really careful about intervening between their realtor and the potential buyer. Of course, no reliable realtors should fail to meet the state's requirement of full disclosure. However it is not necessary to introduce the possibility of offering a property which will give the buyer a front row seat to scenes of horror, featuring gore and dismemberment.

> *Life Lesson:*
>
> *Listen more and speak less.*

Loren Keim's Compelling Buyers to Call

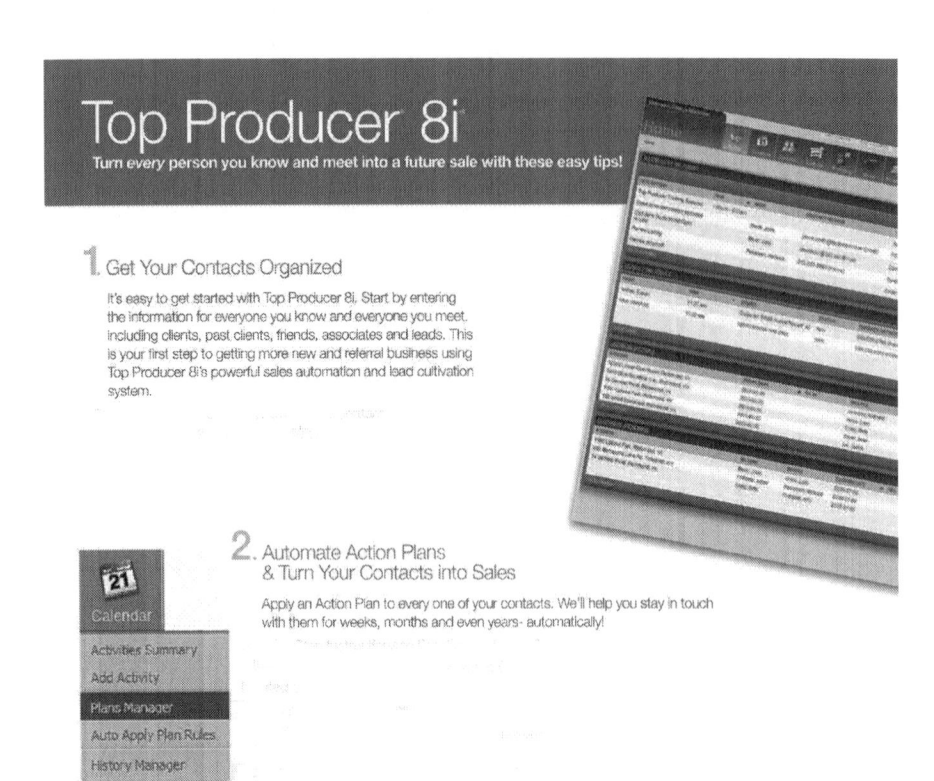

Top Producer 8i
Turn every person you know and meet into a future sale with these easy tips!

1. Get Your Contacts Organized

It's easy to get started with Top Producer 8i. Start by entering the information for everyone you know and everyone you meet, including clients, past clients, friends, associates and leads. This is your first step to getting more new and referral business using Top Producer 8i's powerful sales automation and lead cultivation system.

2. Automate Action Plans & Turn Your Contacts into Sales

Apply an Action Plan to every one of your contacts. We'll help you stay in touch with them for weeks, months and even years - automatically!

3. Get Free Video Training, 24/7

Invest a few minutes a day and learn tips, tricks and best practices to improve your business.

Special Rates for Readers of this book | www.RealEstatesNextLevel.com

Loren Keim's Compelling Buyers to Call

End Notes

[i] Malcolm Gladwell, The Tipping Point: How Little Things Can Make a Big Difference (New York, NY, Back Bay Books, 2002).

[ii] Floyd Wickman is the creator of the Sweathogs real estate training program and others. His training events are listed online at www.floydwickman.com

[iii] Postlets is a registered trademark of Zillow.com

[iv] Spencer Johnson Kenneth Blanchard, Who Moved My Cheese?: An Amazing Way to Deal with Change in Your Work and in Your Life. (New York, NY, G.P. Putnam's Sons, 1998)

[v] Price Pritchett, You Squared: A High Velocity Formula for Multiplying Your Personal Effectiveness in Quantum Leaps (Dallas, TX: Pritchett & Associates, 2007) p 3.

[vi] Joe Stumpf is the creator of The Main Event real estate training program and has developed a system of building business by referral. His training events are listed online at www.byreferralonly.com.

[vii] Courtesy of Gooder Group. www.GooderGroup.com, Fairfax, Virginia

[viii] Facebook is a registered trademark of Facebook, Inc.

[ix] Myspace is a registered trademark of Myspace, Inc.

Loren Keim's Compelling Buyers to Call

[x] National Association of Realtors Profile of Home Buyers and Sellers 2010.

[xi] Dr. Denis Waitley, <u>The Seeds of Greatness</u> (Berkley, 1986).

Dr. Denis Waitley, <u>The Psychology of Winning</u> (London Cedar, 1987).

Realtor.com is a trademark of "operated by National Association of REALTORS"
Trulia is a trademark of Trulia, Inc.
Zillow is a trademark of Zillow, Inc.
Yahoo Real Estate is a trademark of Yahoo! Inc.
Homes.com is a trademark of Dominion Enterprises
Century21.com is a trademark of Century 21 Real Estate LLC
Re/Max.com is a trademark of RE/MAX LLC
ColdwellBanker.com is a trademark of CBRELLC
FrontDoor.com is a trademark of Scripps Networks, LLC
OpenHouse.com is a trademark of Scripps Networks, LLC
HomeFinder.com is a trademark of Classified Ventures, LLC
Powerpoint is a registered trademark of Microsoft
iPad is a registered trademark of Apple